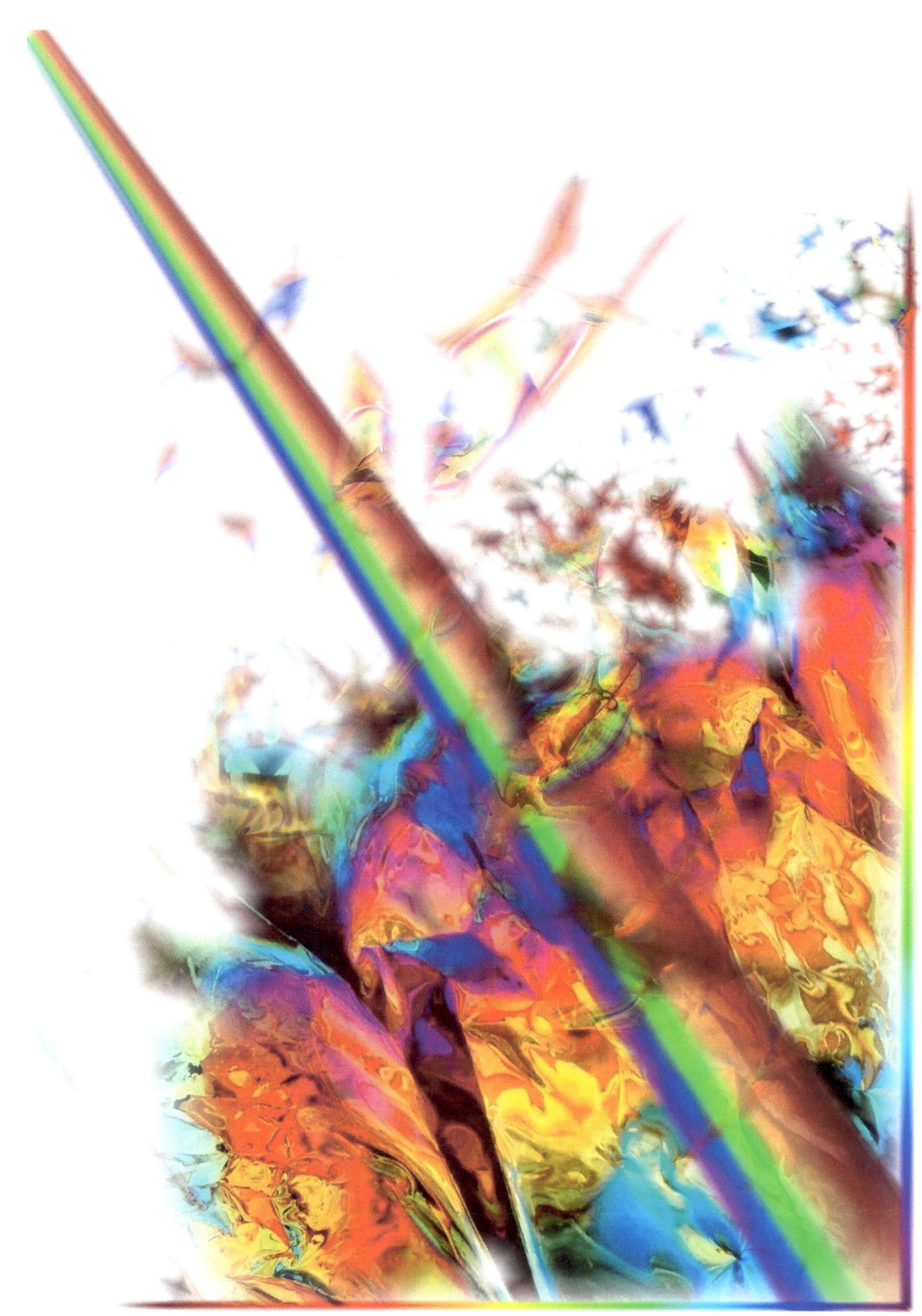

Artisan of Light: 2016

A unique abstract art form

Robert B. Calkins

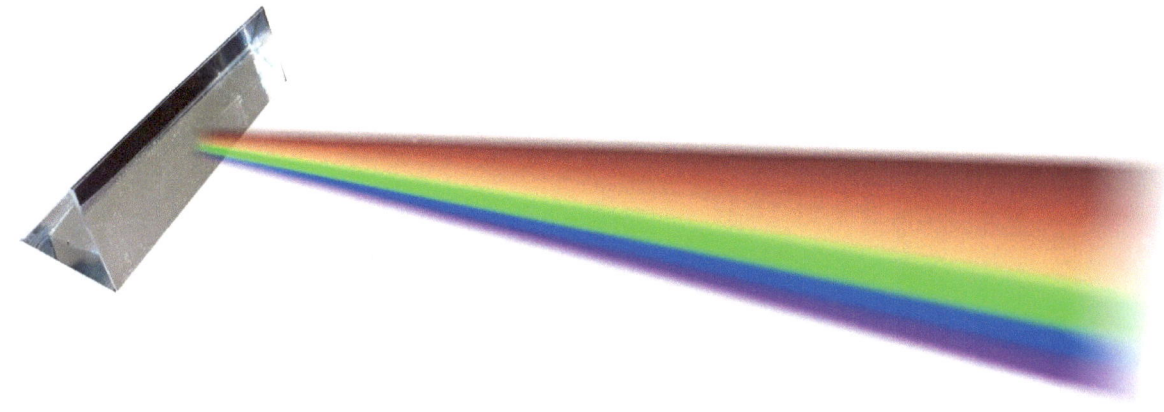

Published by Robert B. Calkins
Issaquah, WA

Printed by CreateSpace

Calkins, Robert B.
  Art, Abstract, Sunlight, Art form, Integral.

ISBN-13: 978-1542700023

Edition 1.0

https://www.amazon.com/author/robertbcalkins

Cover art and design by Robert B. Calkins

Artisan of Light   My award winning art begins with sun light, the source of energy that powers all life on earth. It represents the vitality and exuberance of life itself. My work/play attempts to capture that exuberance and its variety.

My palette is an array of glass prisms which creates the rich colors of the rainbow. Adjusting the individual prisms makes additional color combinations beyond the normal rainbow of a single prism. Using lens, filters, reflections, foam board, glue, paint, overhead transparencies and other objects I create various light effects and take digital photographs of the results. The final process involves using a computer to manipulate the images (such as crop, cut, paste, etc.). I classify my art as mostly non-representational abstract mixed media.

My process and tools were developed over a number of years of experimentation, a sample of which is shown in below.

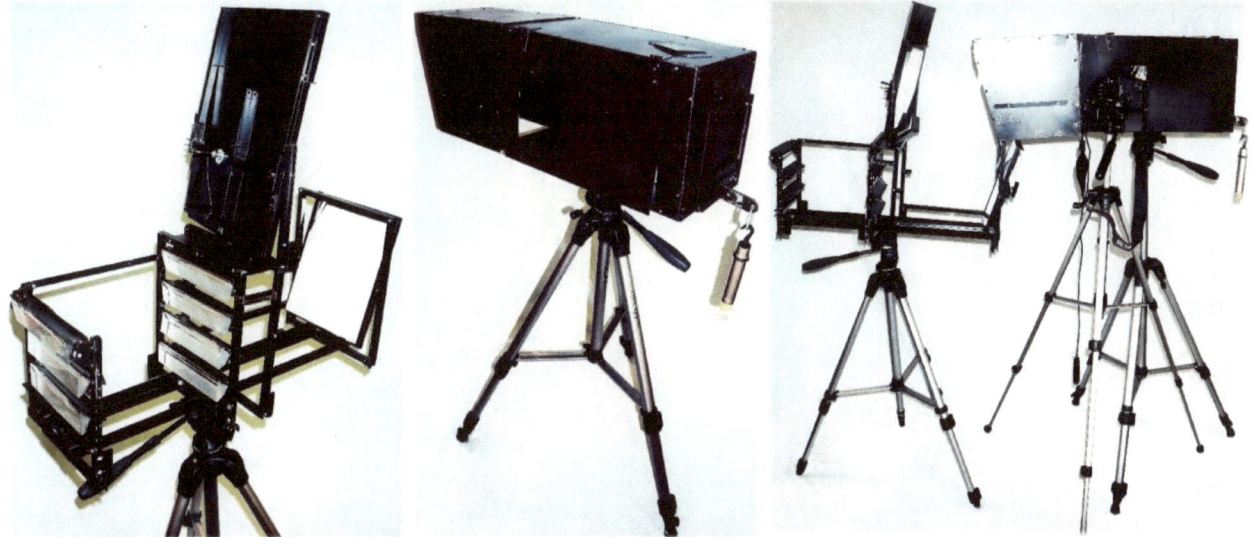

The sunbeam "Ray Slinger"   The "Ray Catcher"   Typical art project set up

One irony of this art form is that it starts with sun light and I not only live in the Pacific Northwest but in heavily forested woods. The only time of the year I can get appropriate sun in my studio is on sunny mornings between 9 am and 11 am, late May through August. My response to this obstacle has been to make my studio mobile. When the sun is shining but not in my studio, I take my show on the road to find a sunny spot to set up the portable studio. One favorite spot is the top floor of park-and-ride garages (photo below).

In addition to my art, I am interested in integral philosophy and have authored a book. I have two bachelors and two master's degrees and am retired from a career in aerospace R&D.

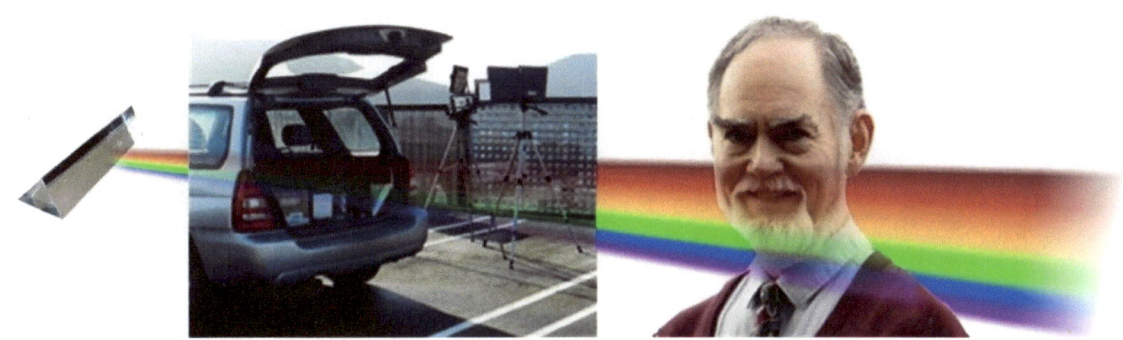

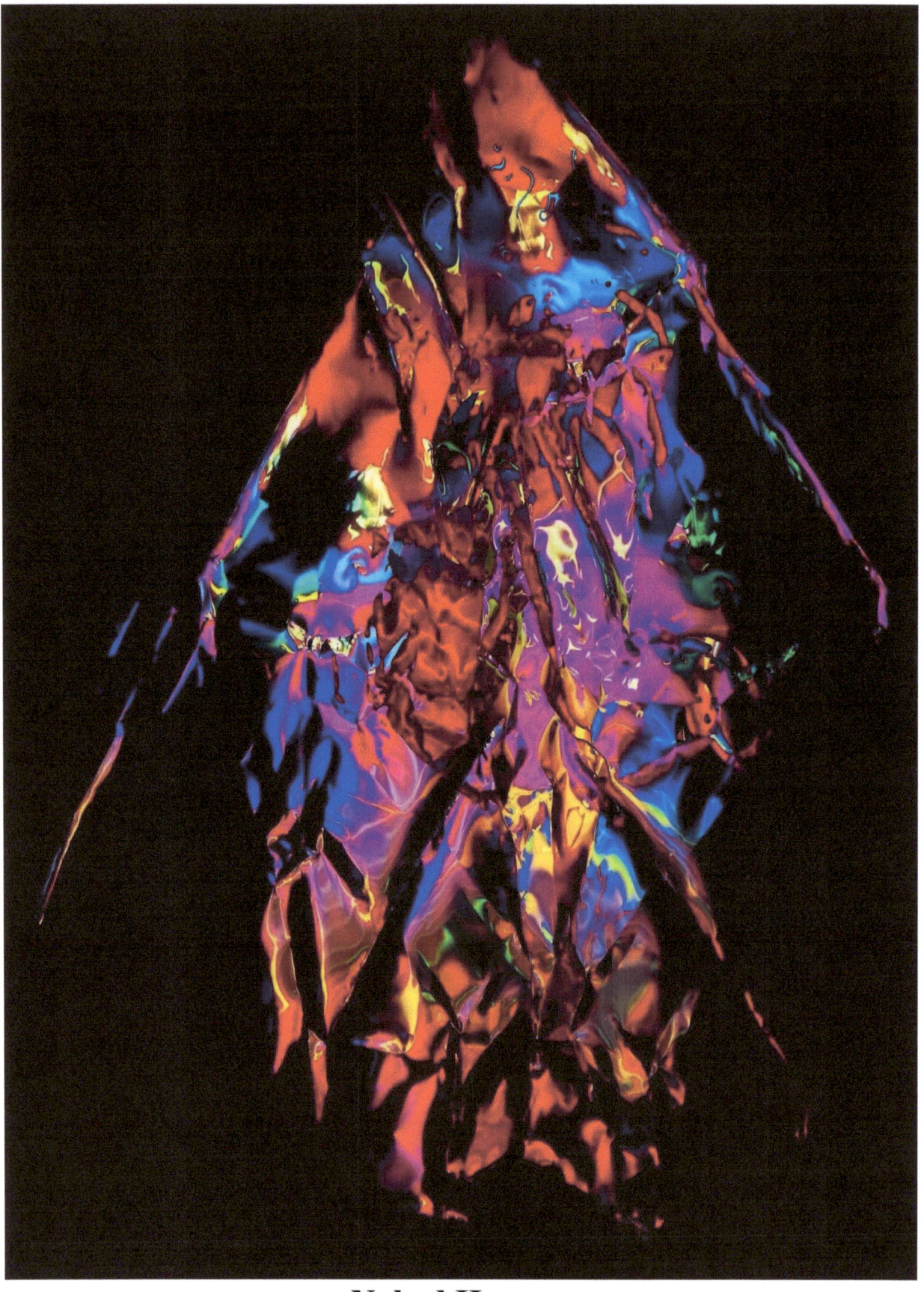

Naked Hunger

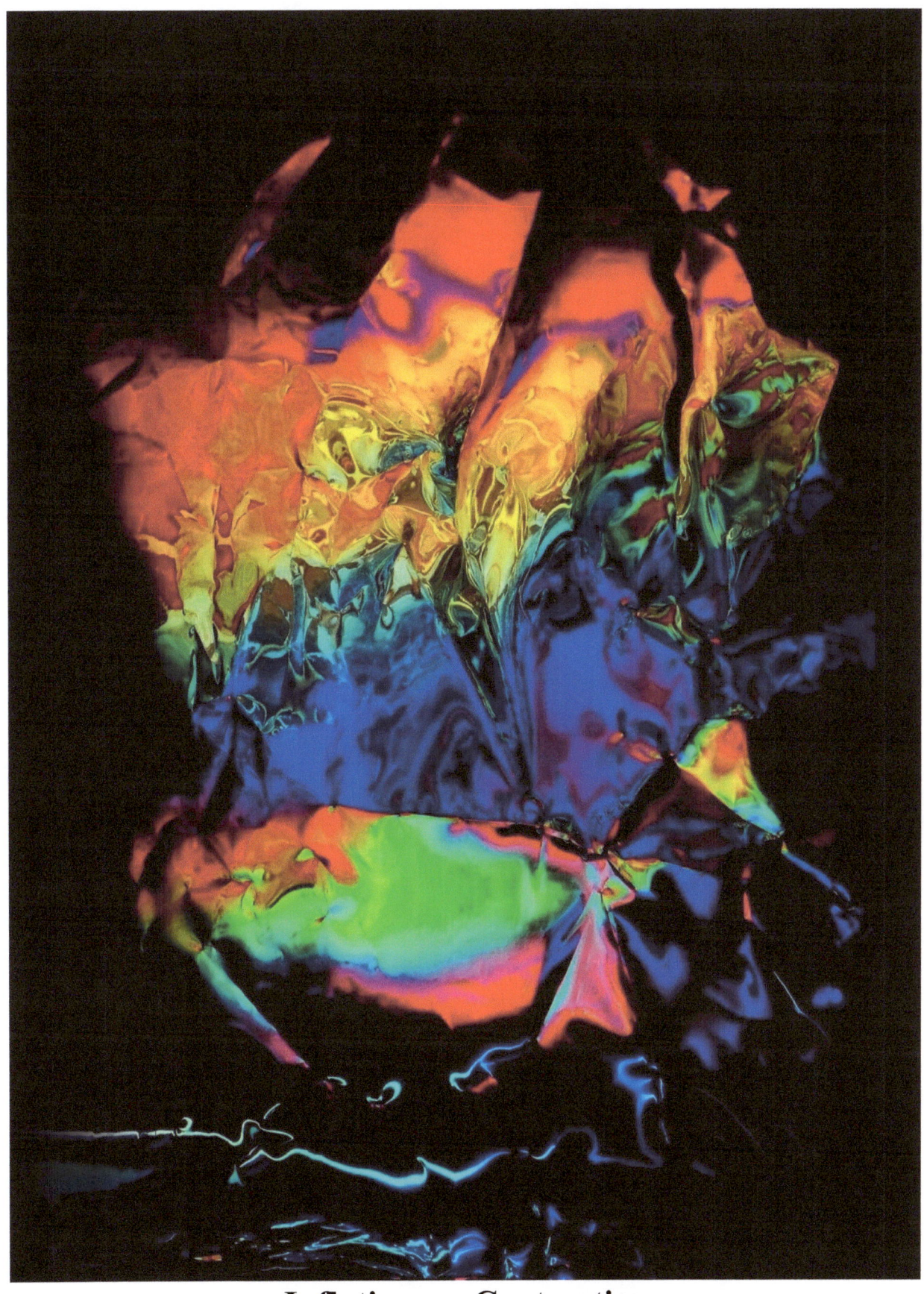

Inflationary Contraction

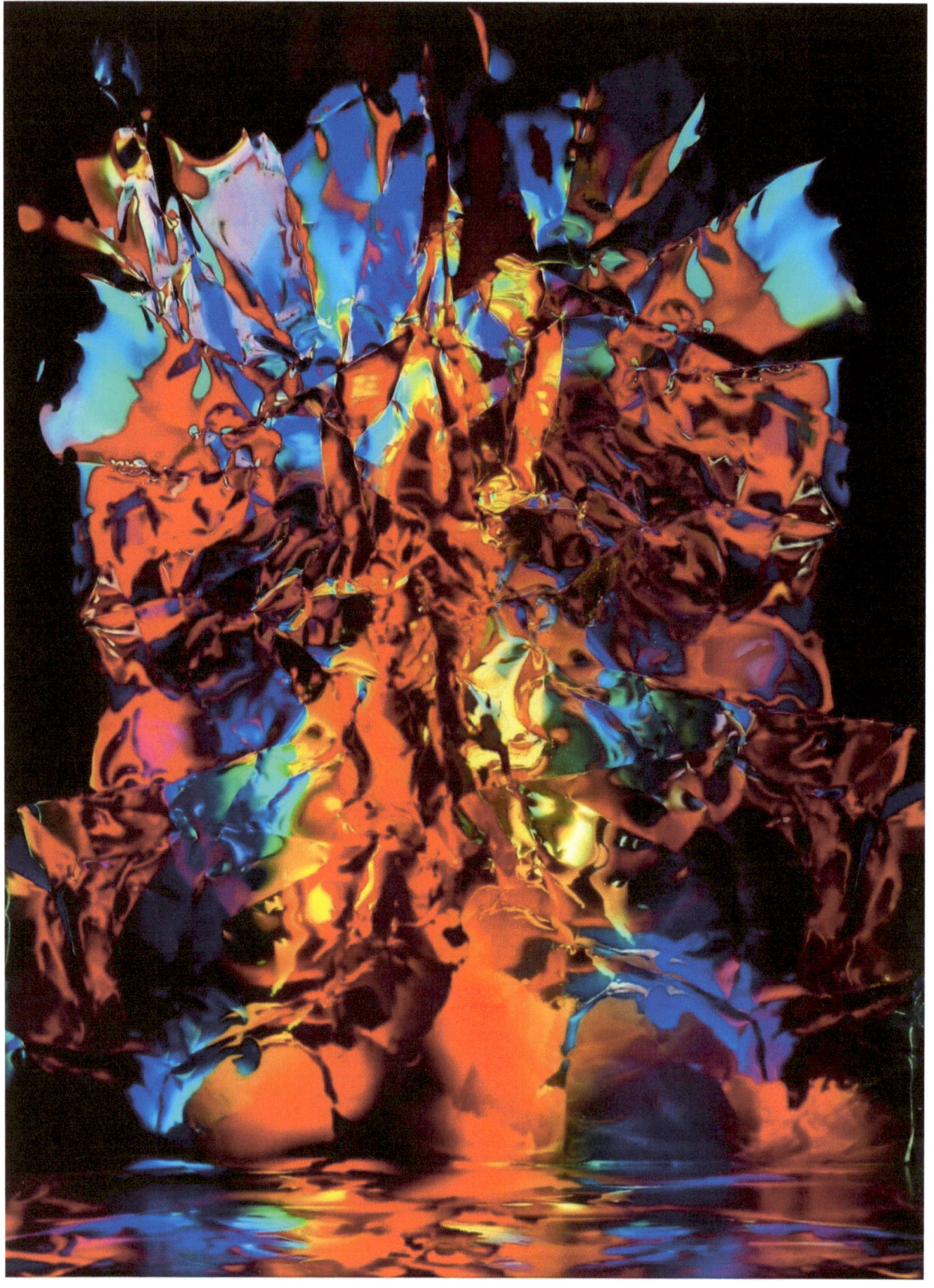

Attention Disorder Deficit

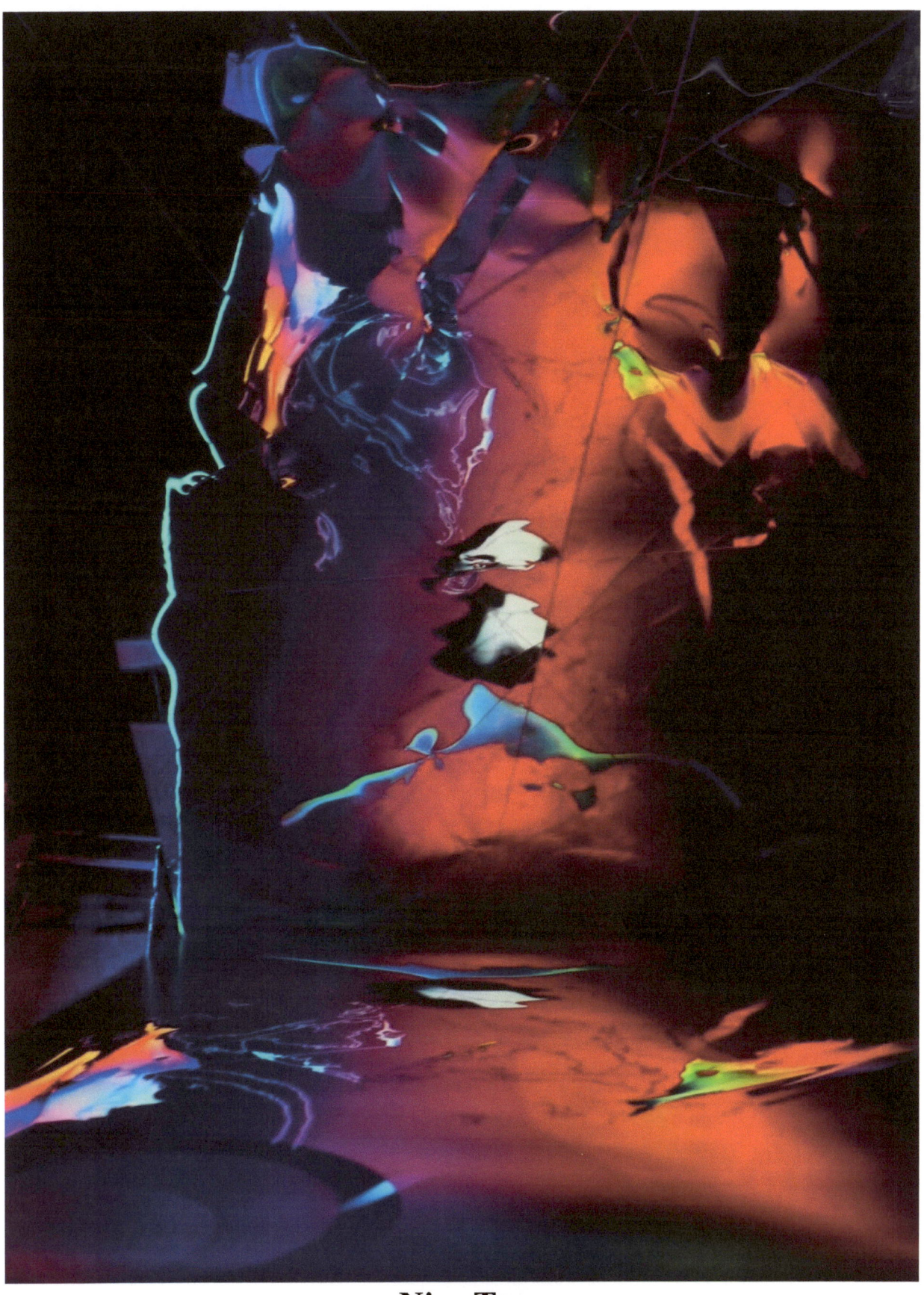

Nice Try

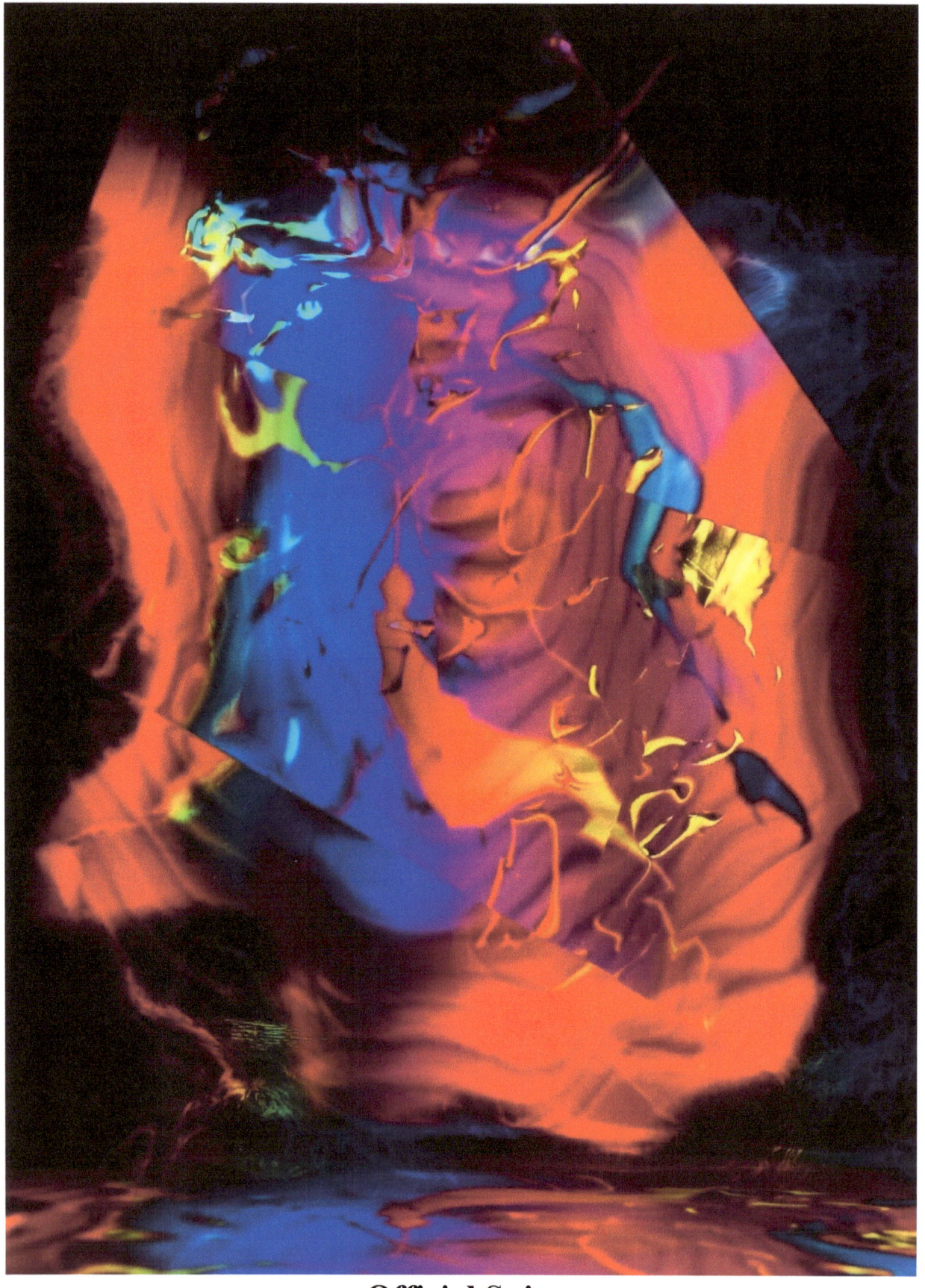

Official Spin

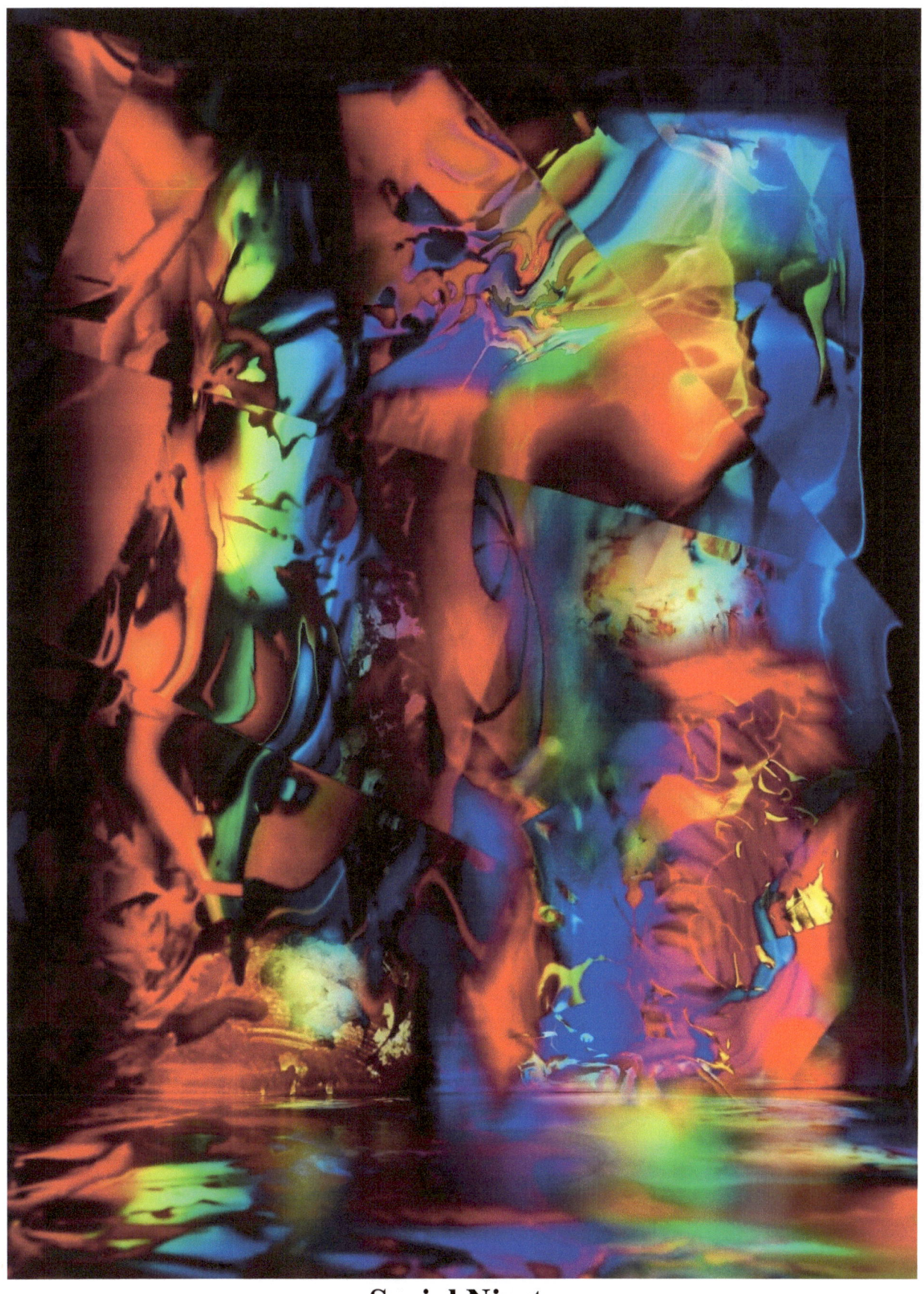

Social Nicety

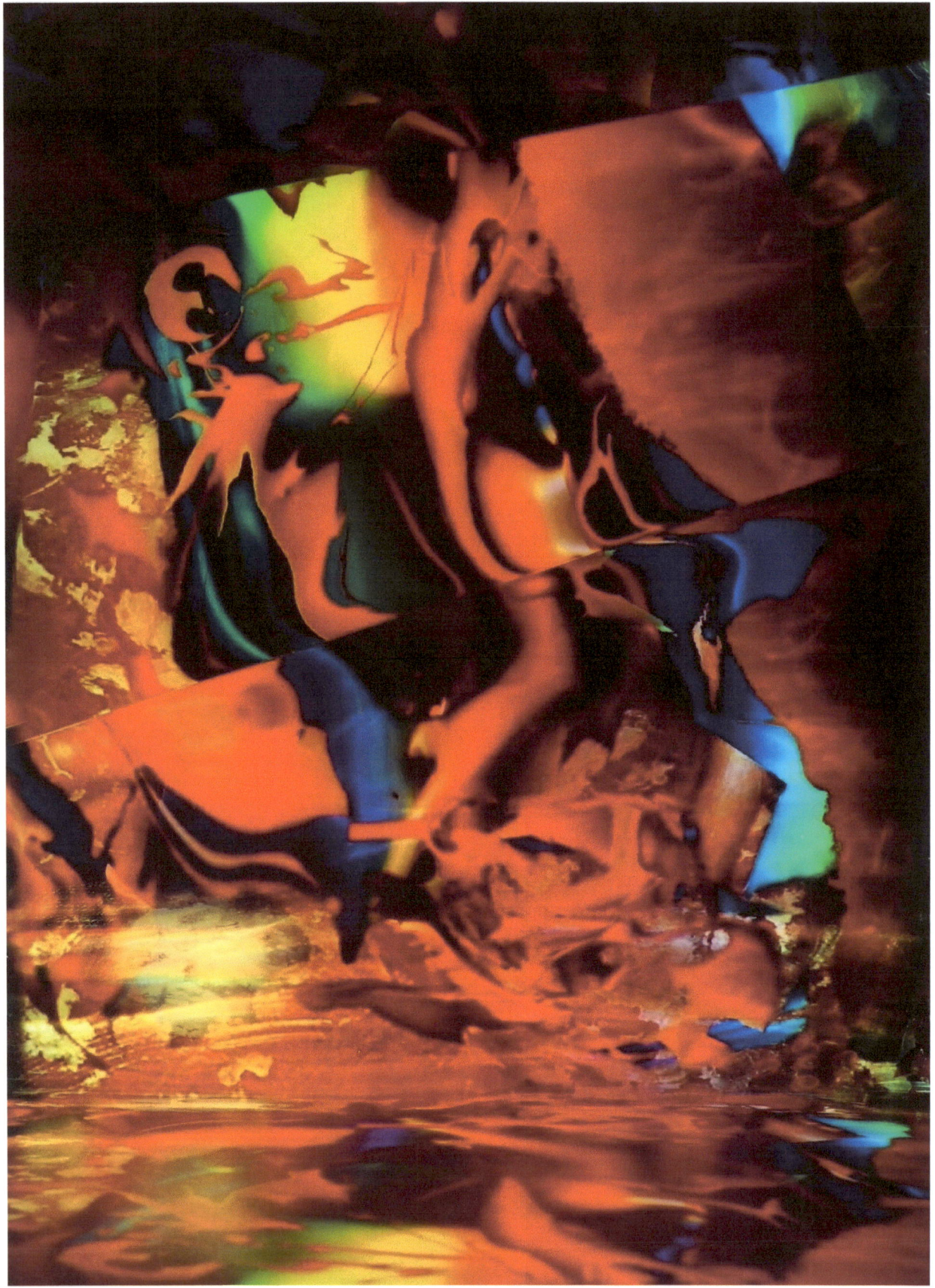

This Is The Title

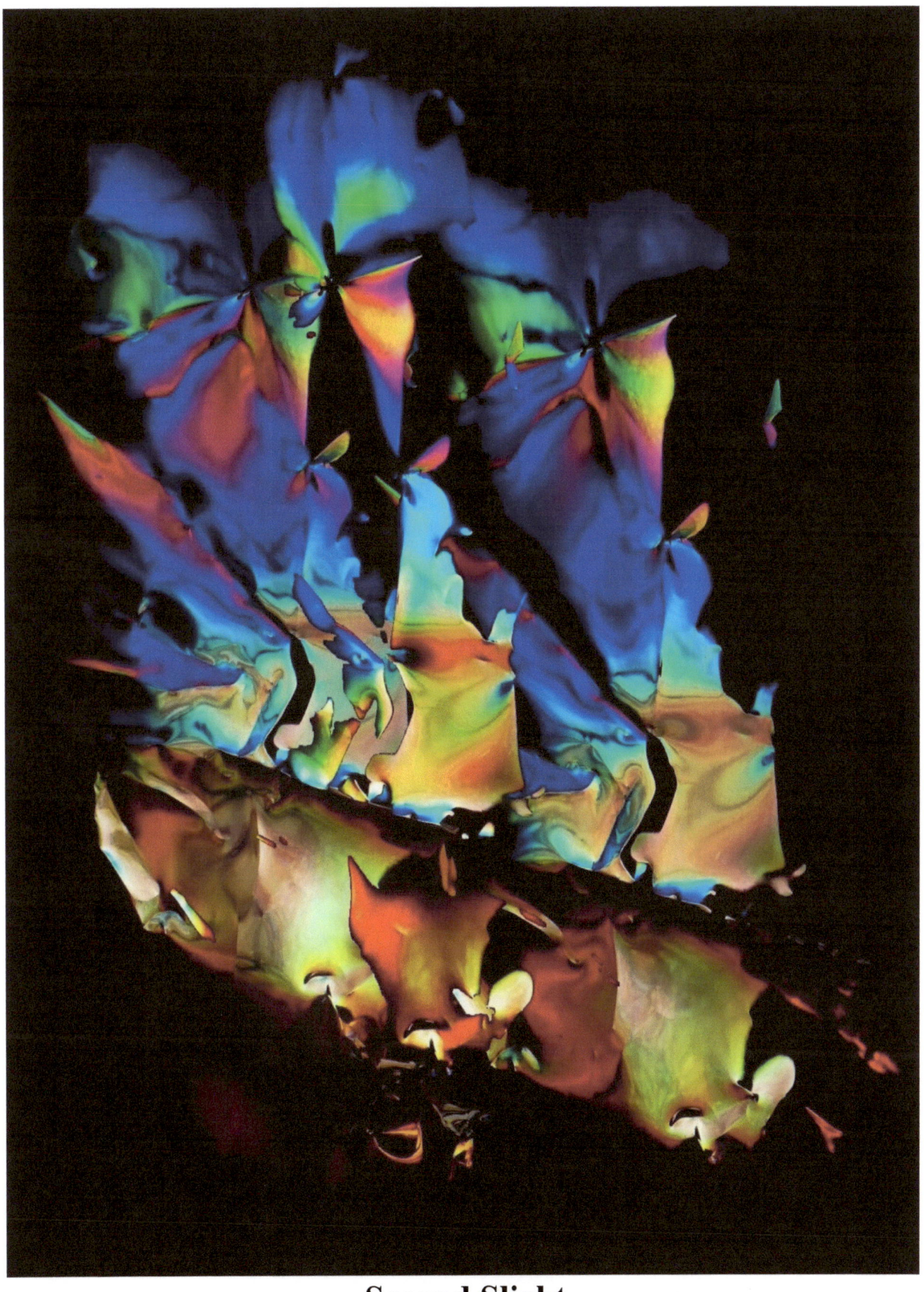

Second Slight

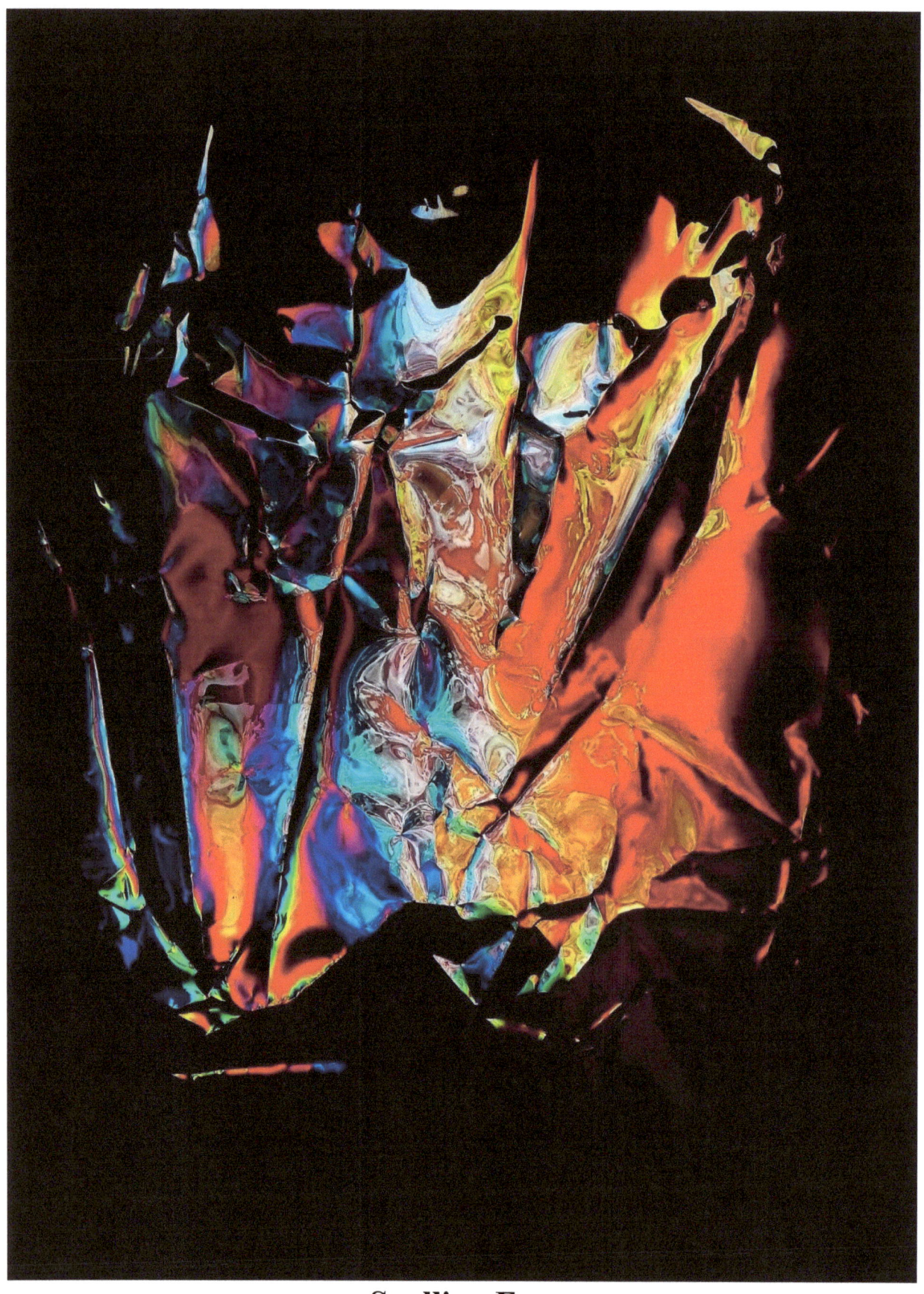

Spelling Era

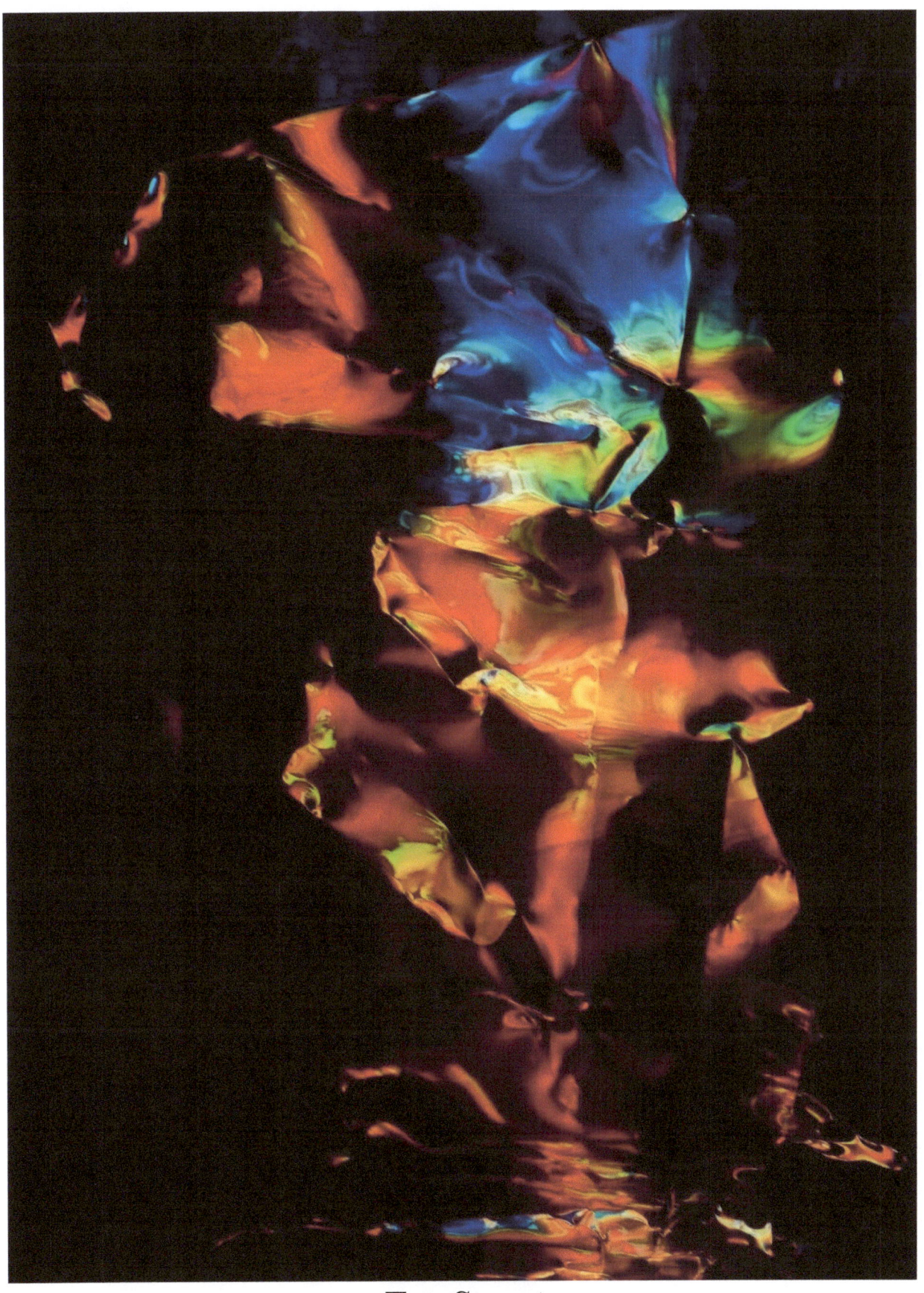

Top Secret

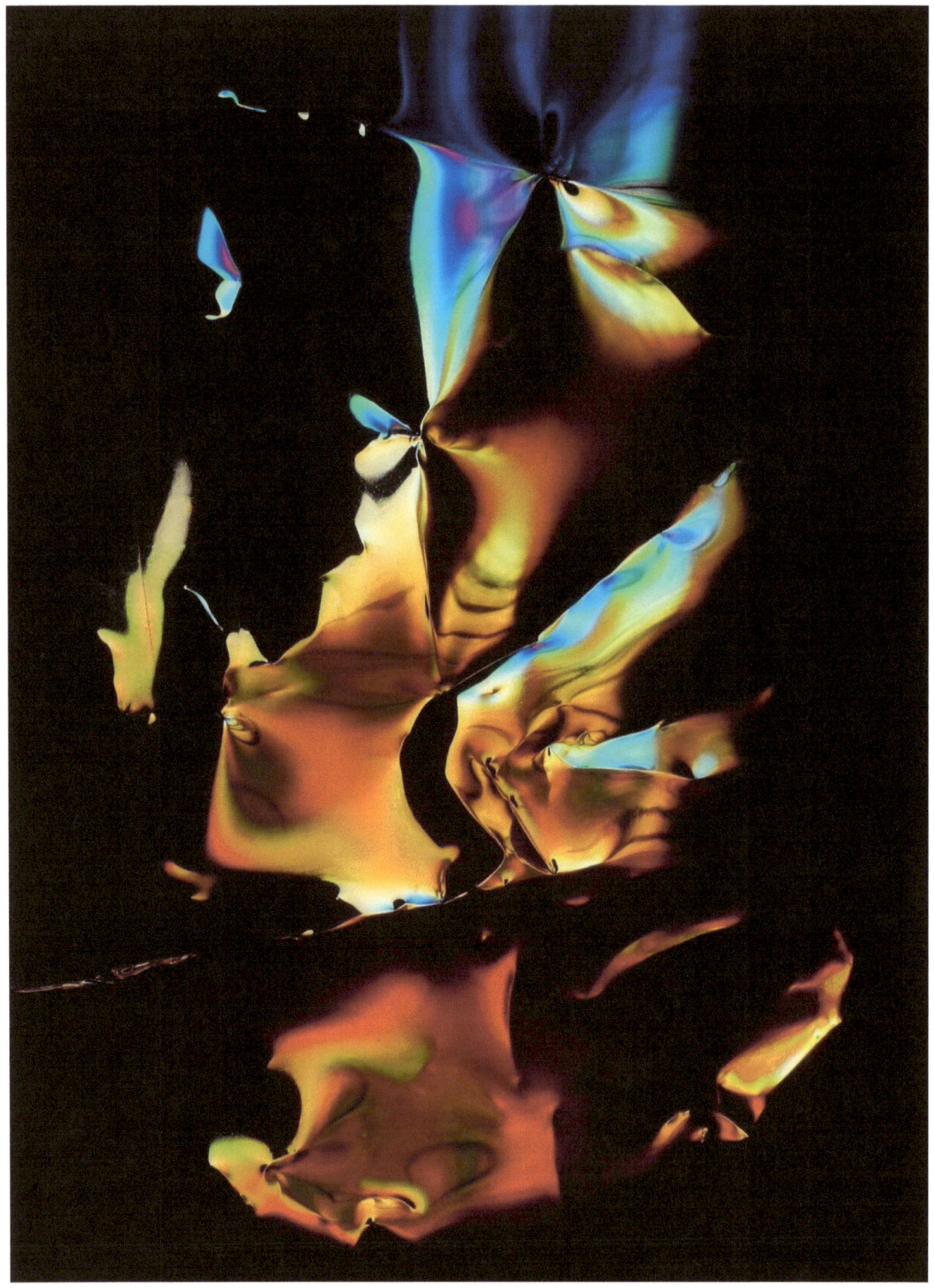

Presidential Blunder

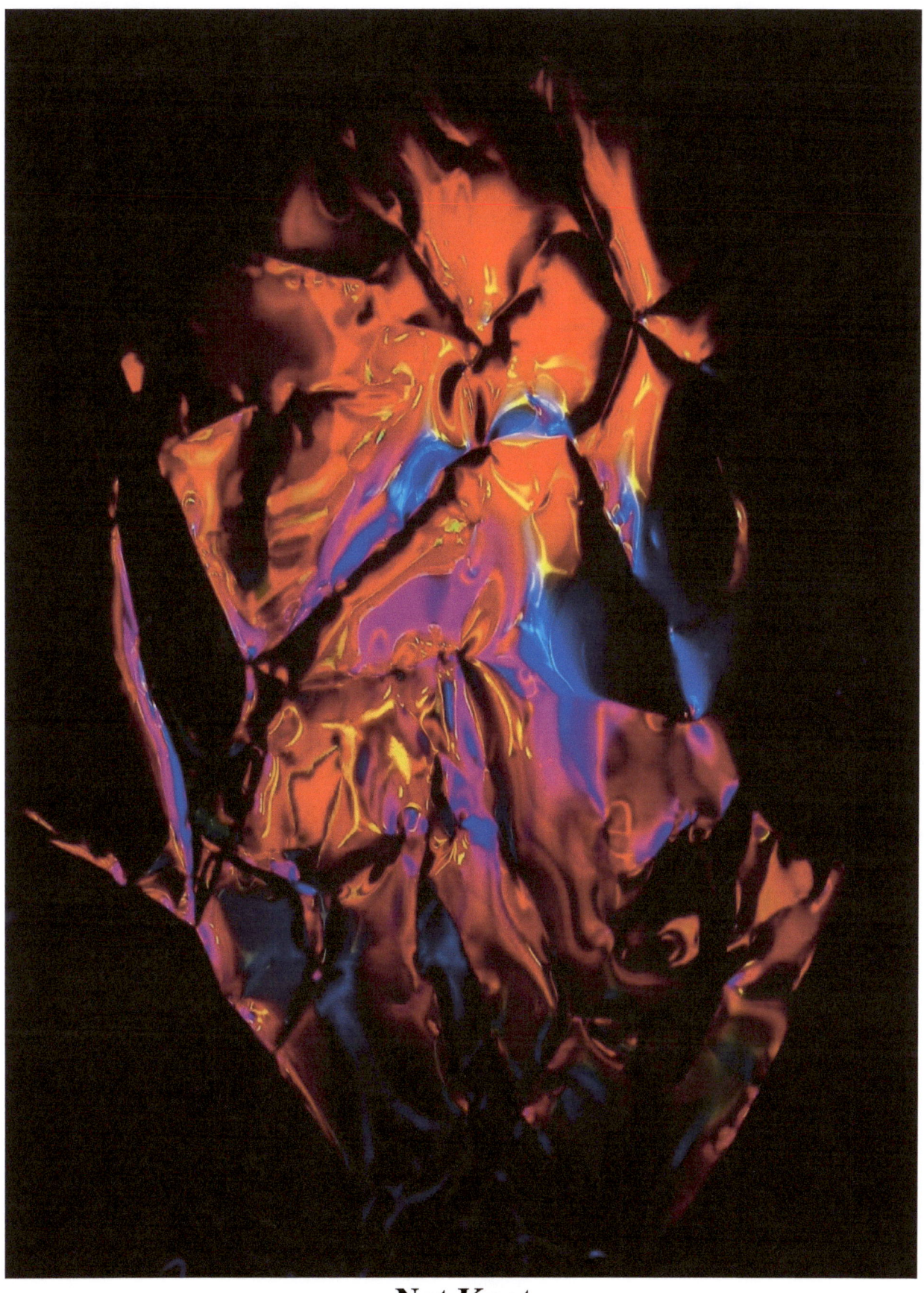

Not Knot

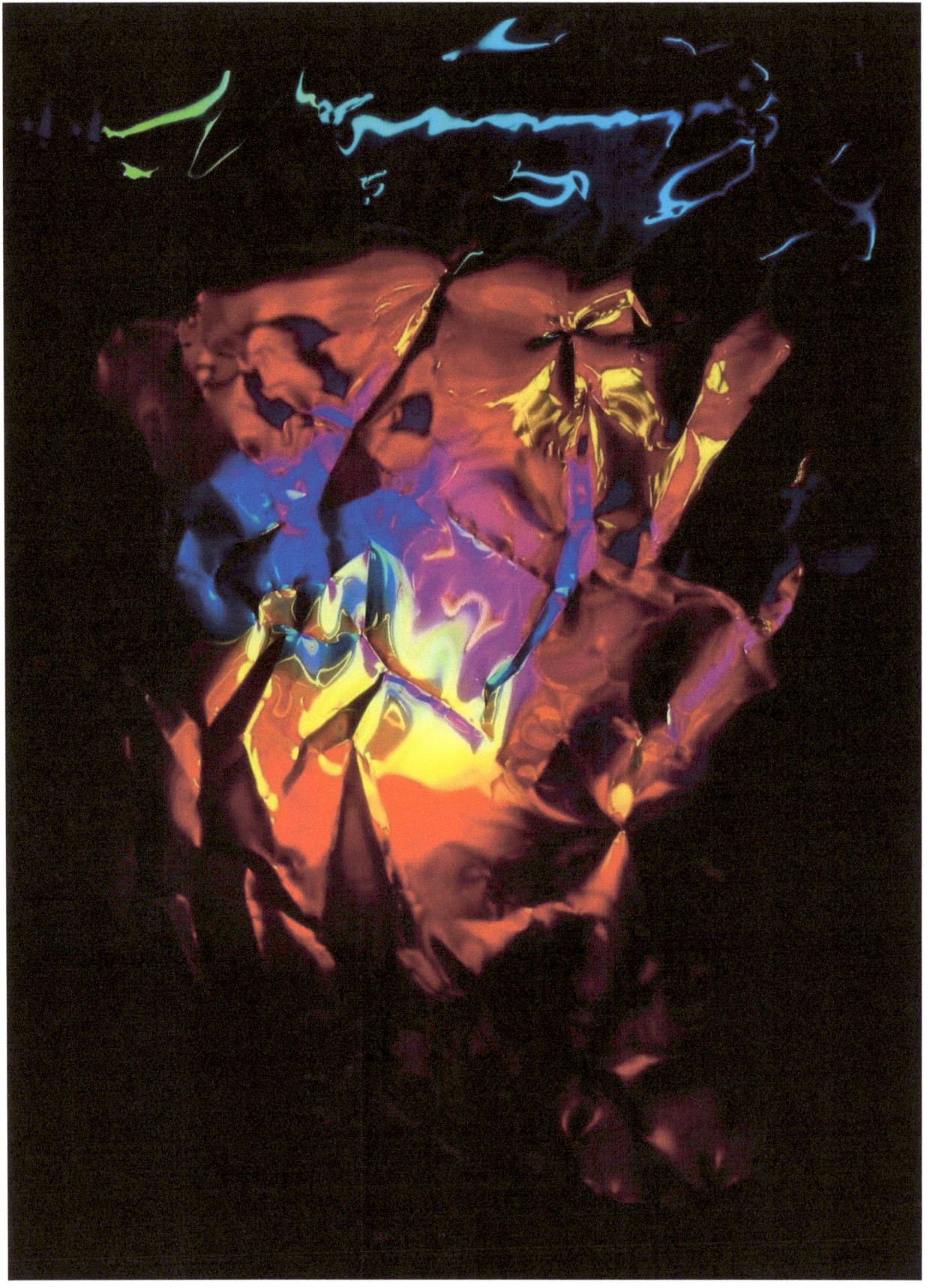

Well, I Don't Know

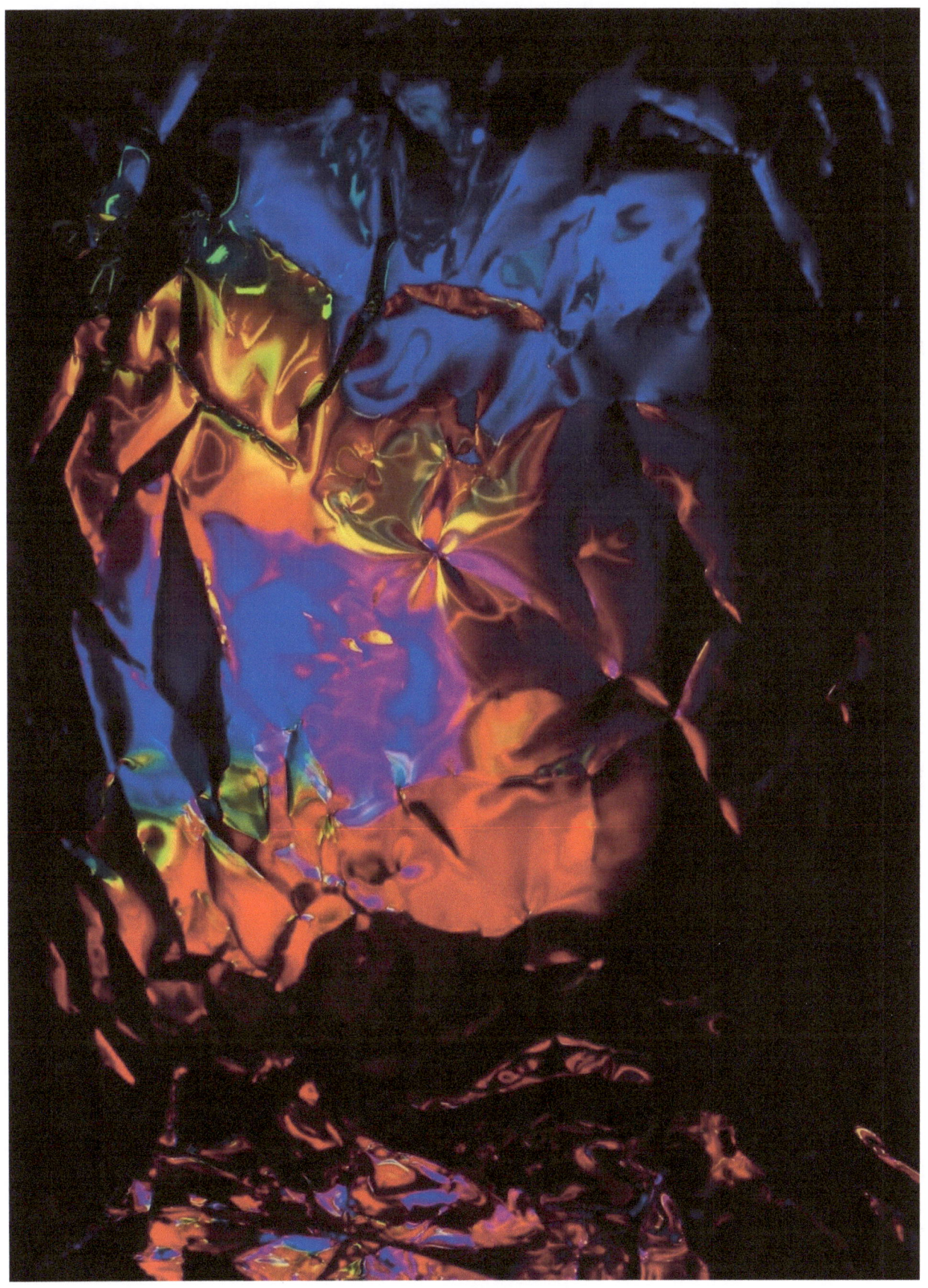

Twus Not

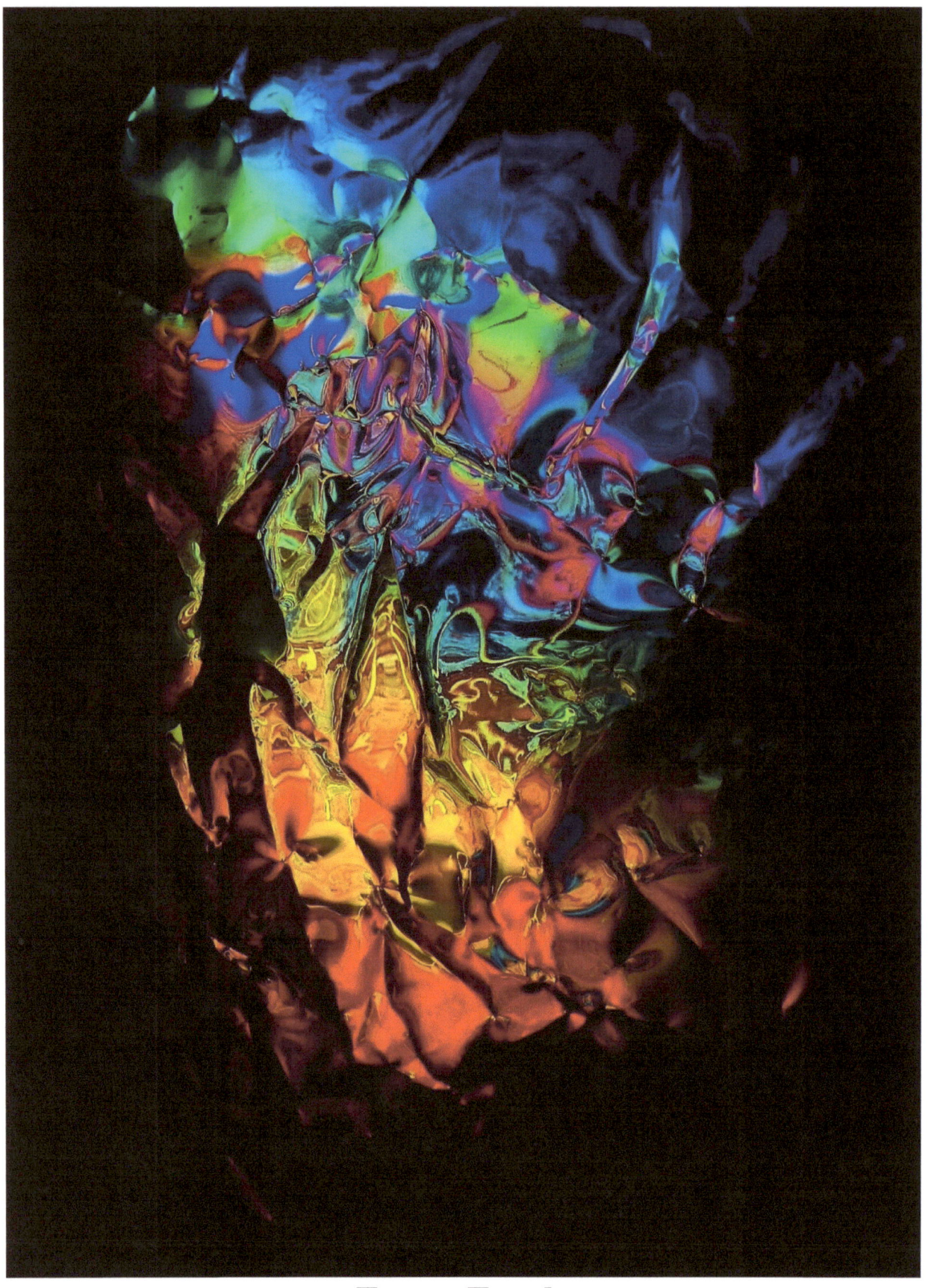

Tantra Tangle

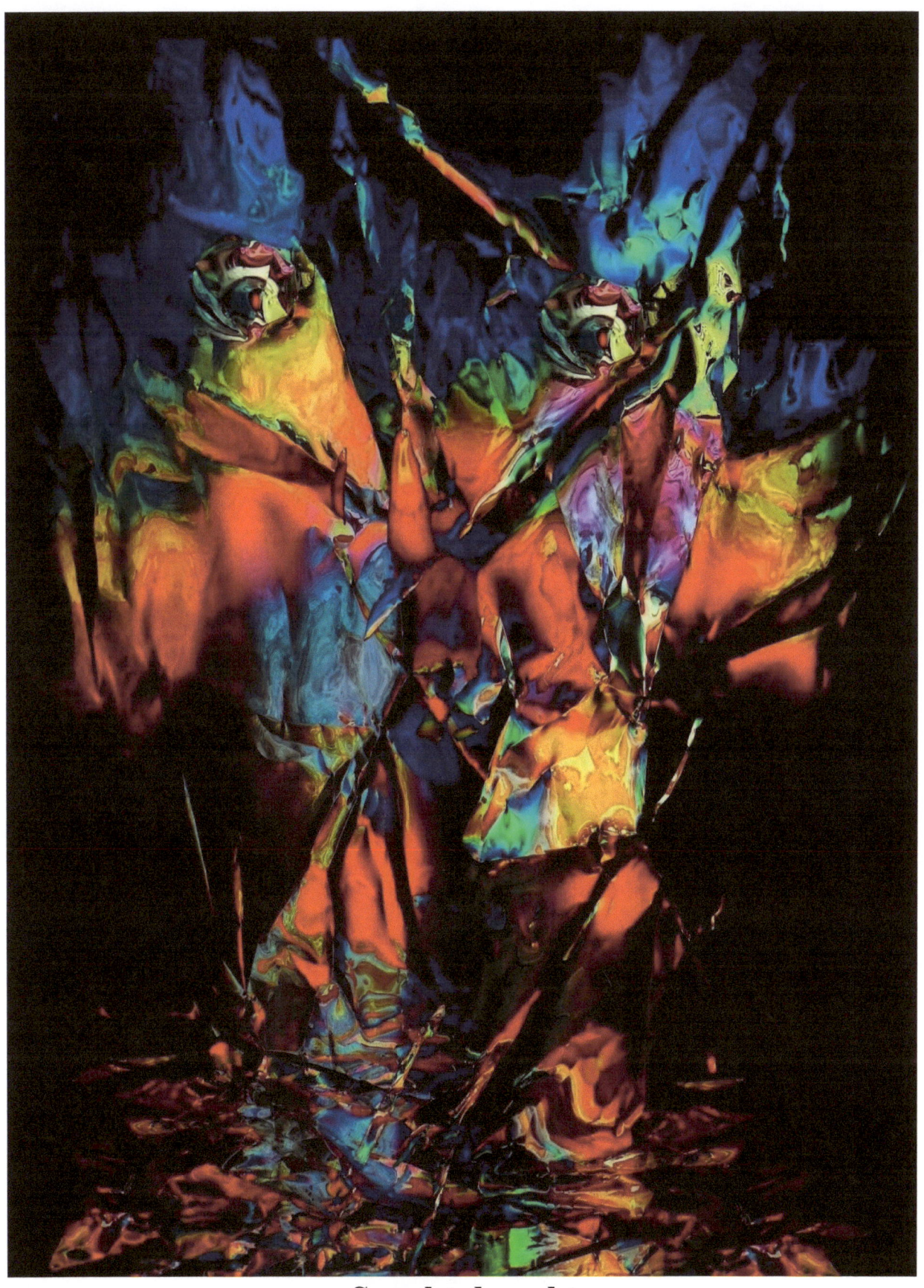

Soughtnbought

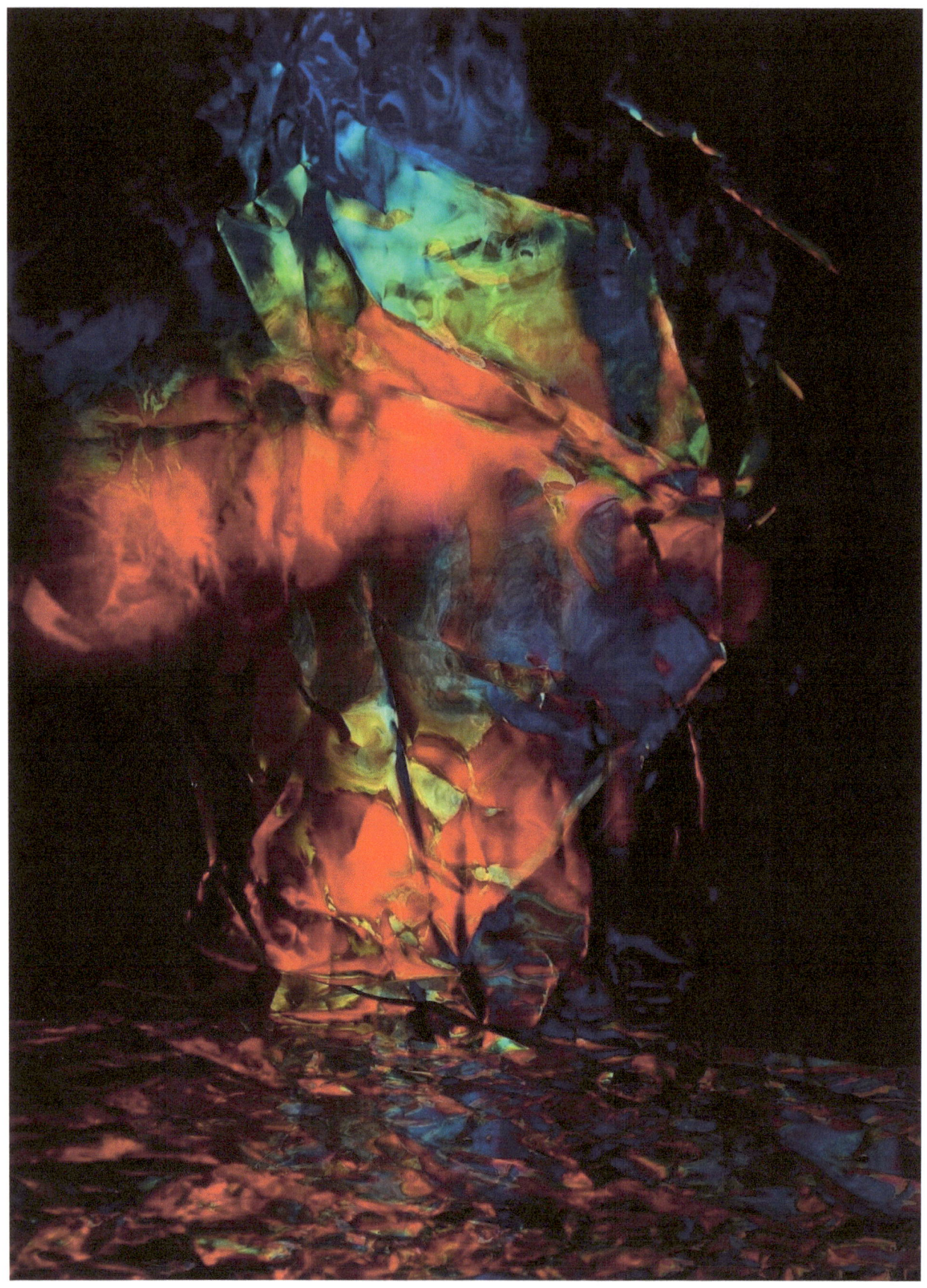

Slip and Thrust

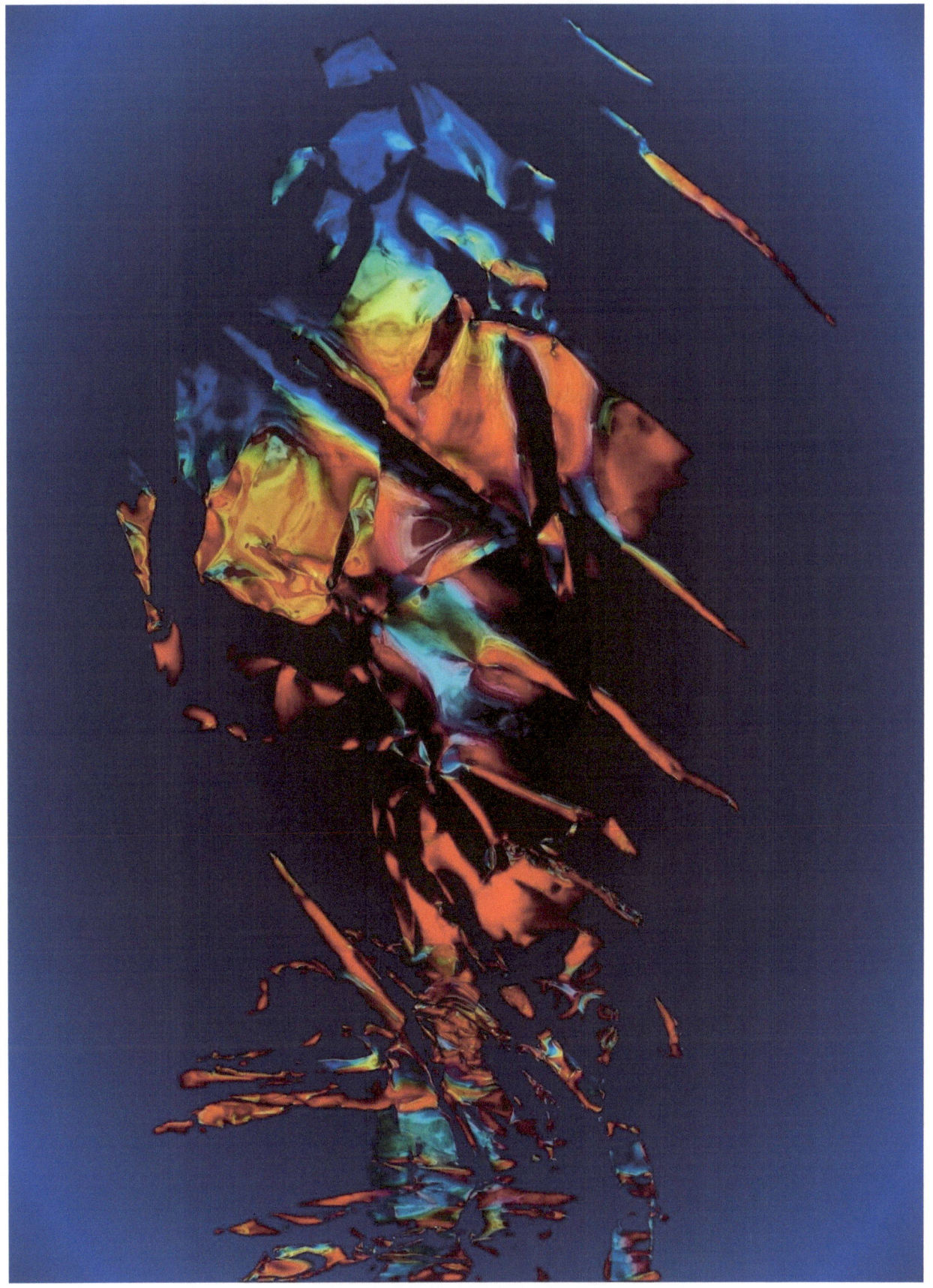

Rhombus Omnibus

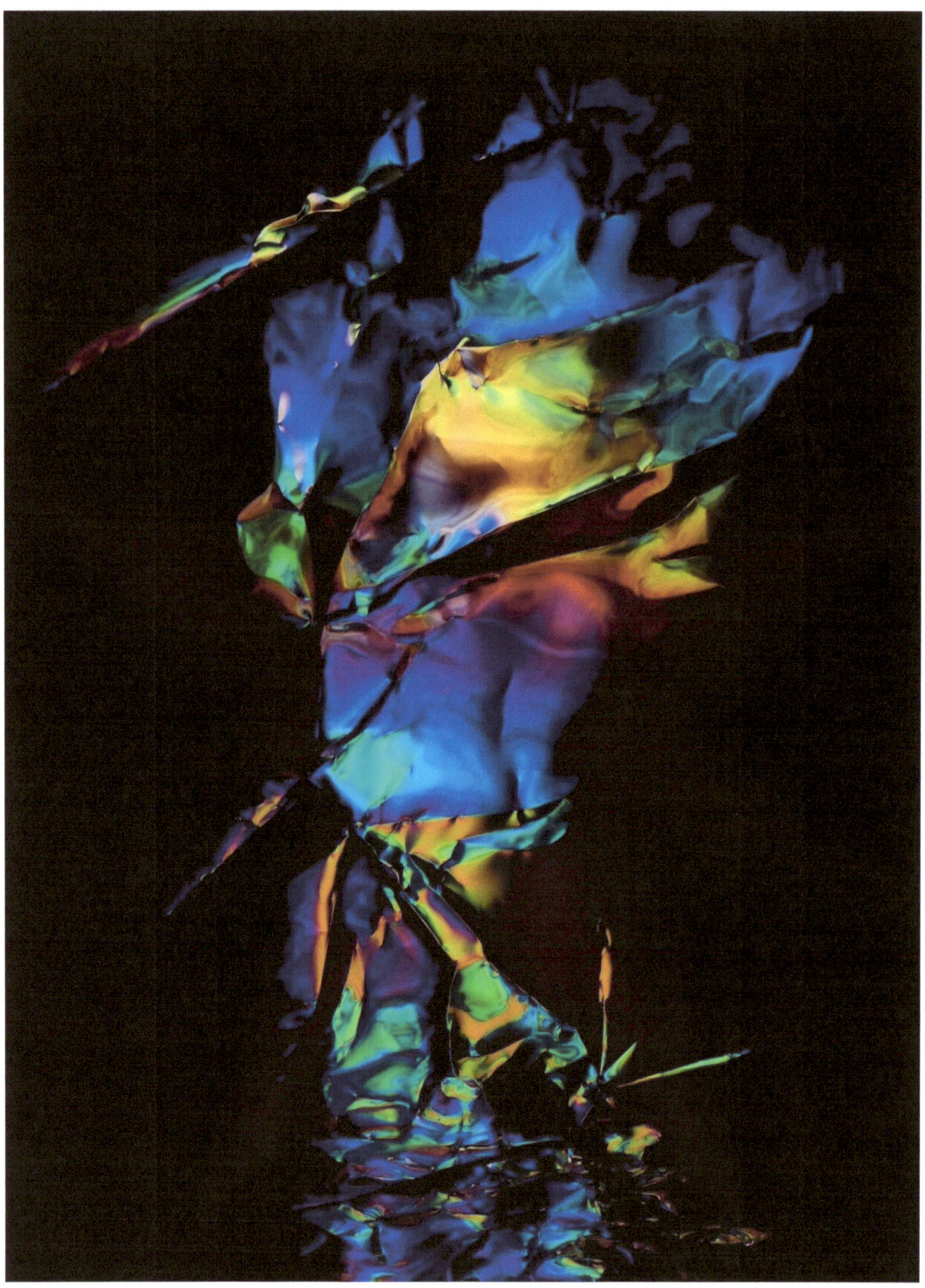

33 Titles

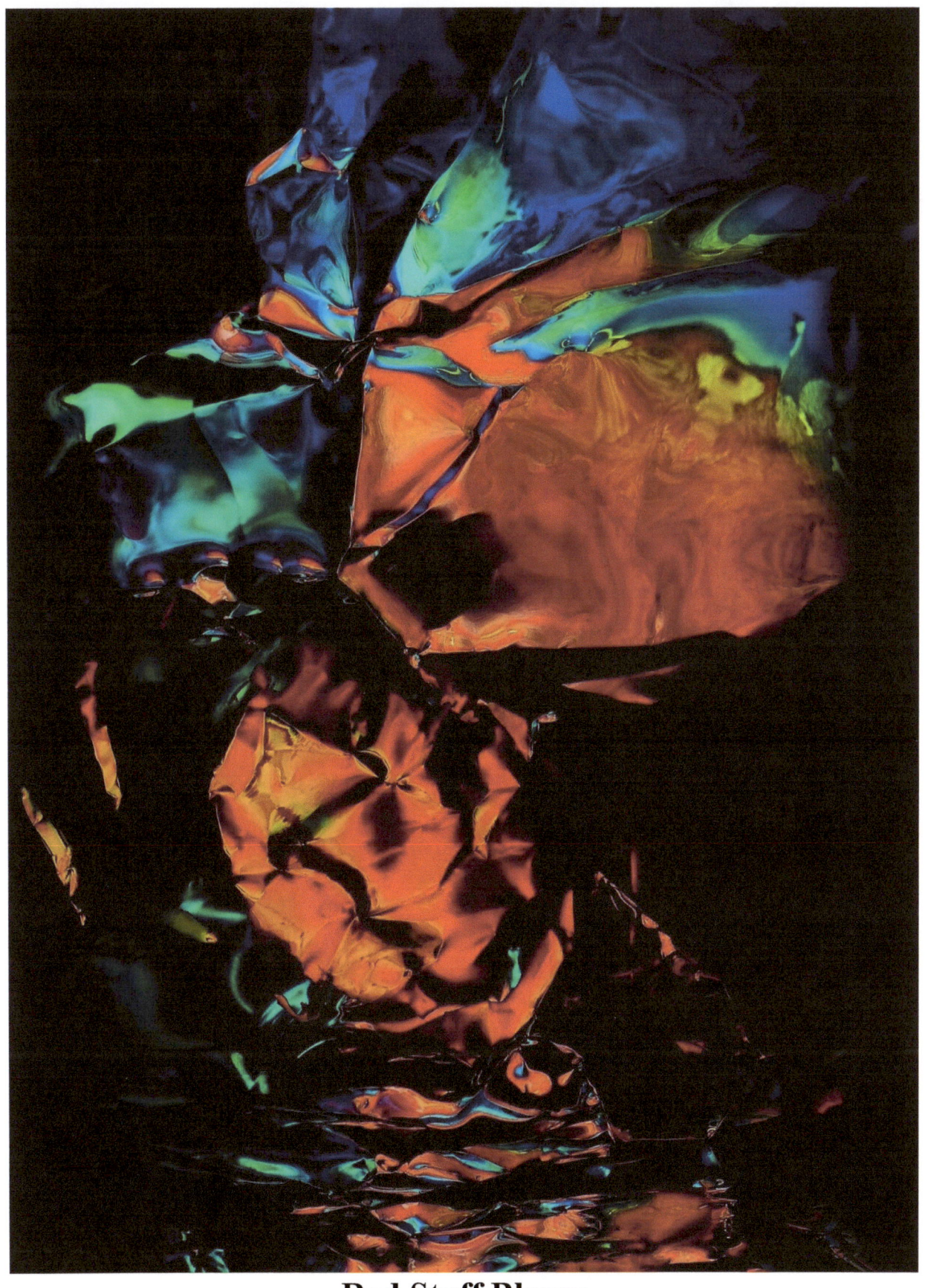

Red Stuff Blurge

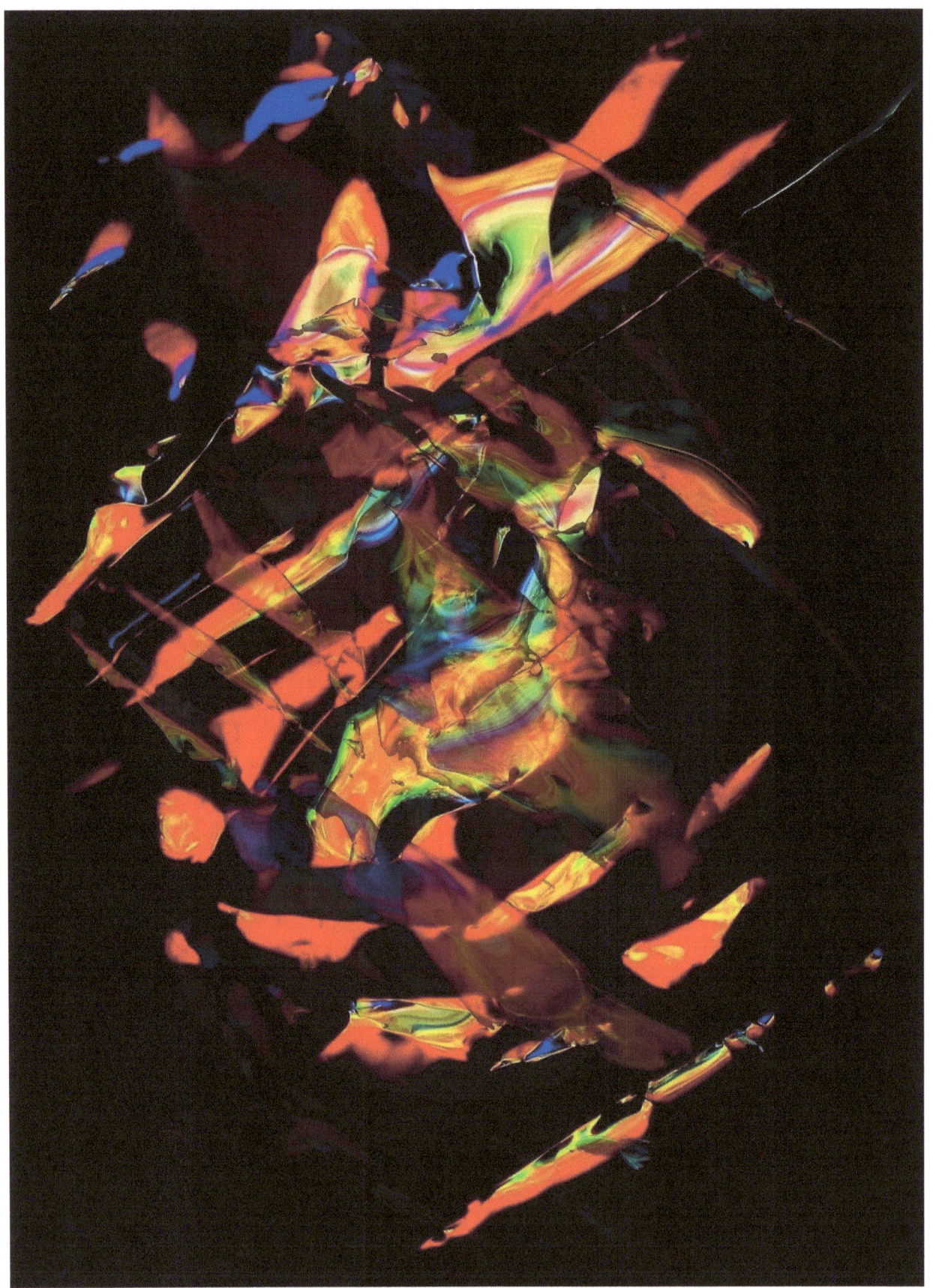

Aileron Roll

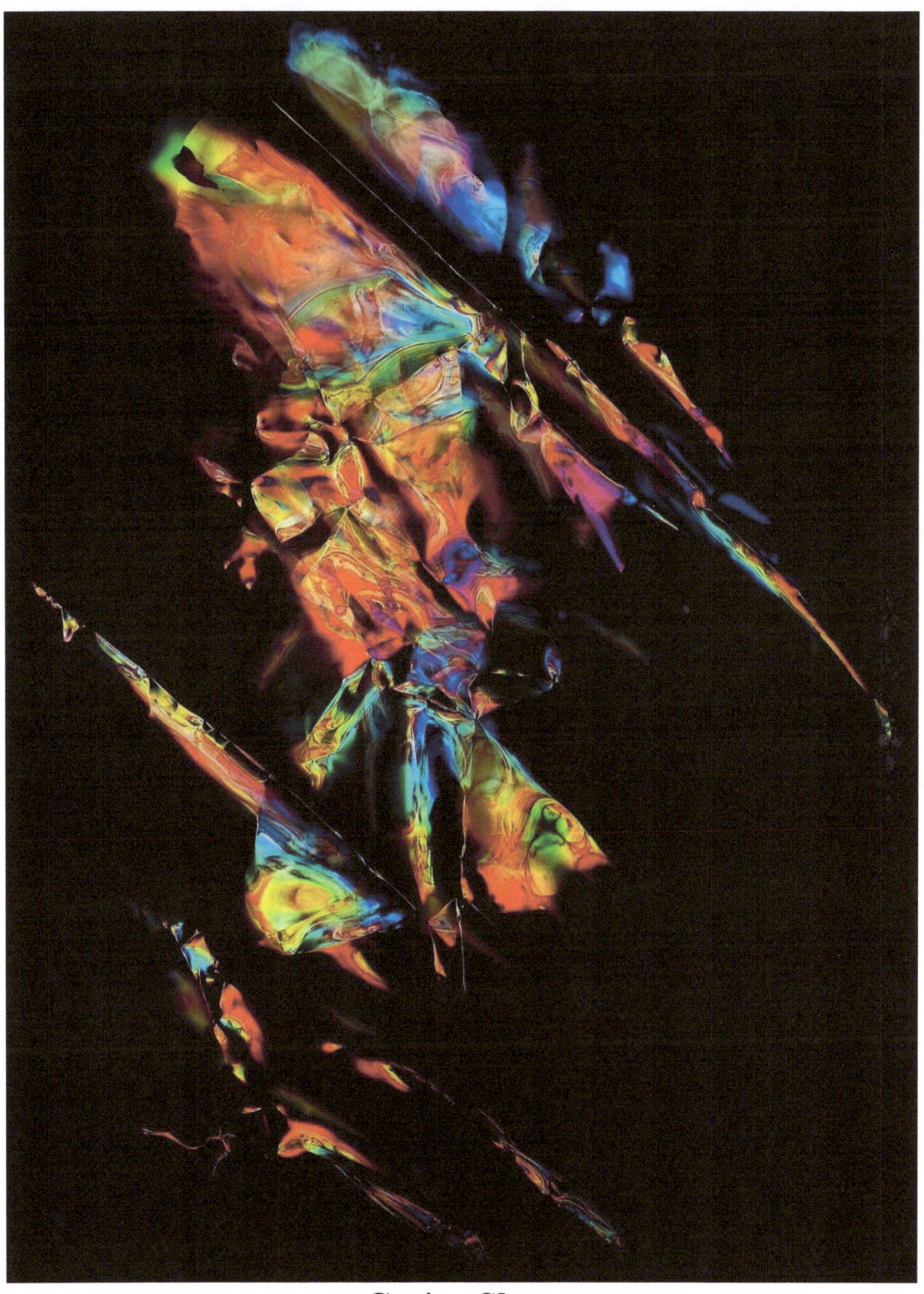

Crying Sham

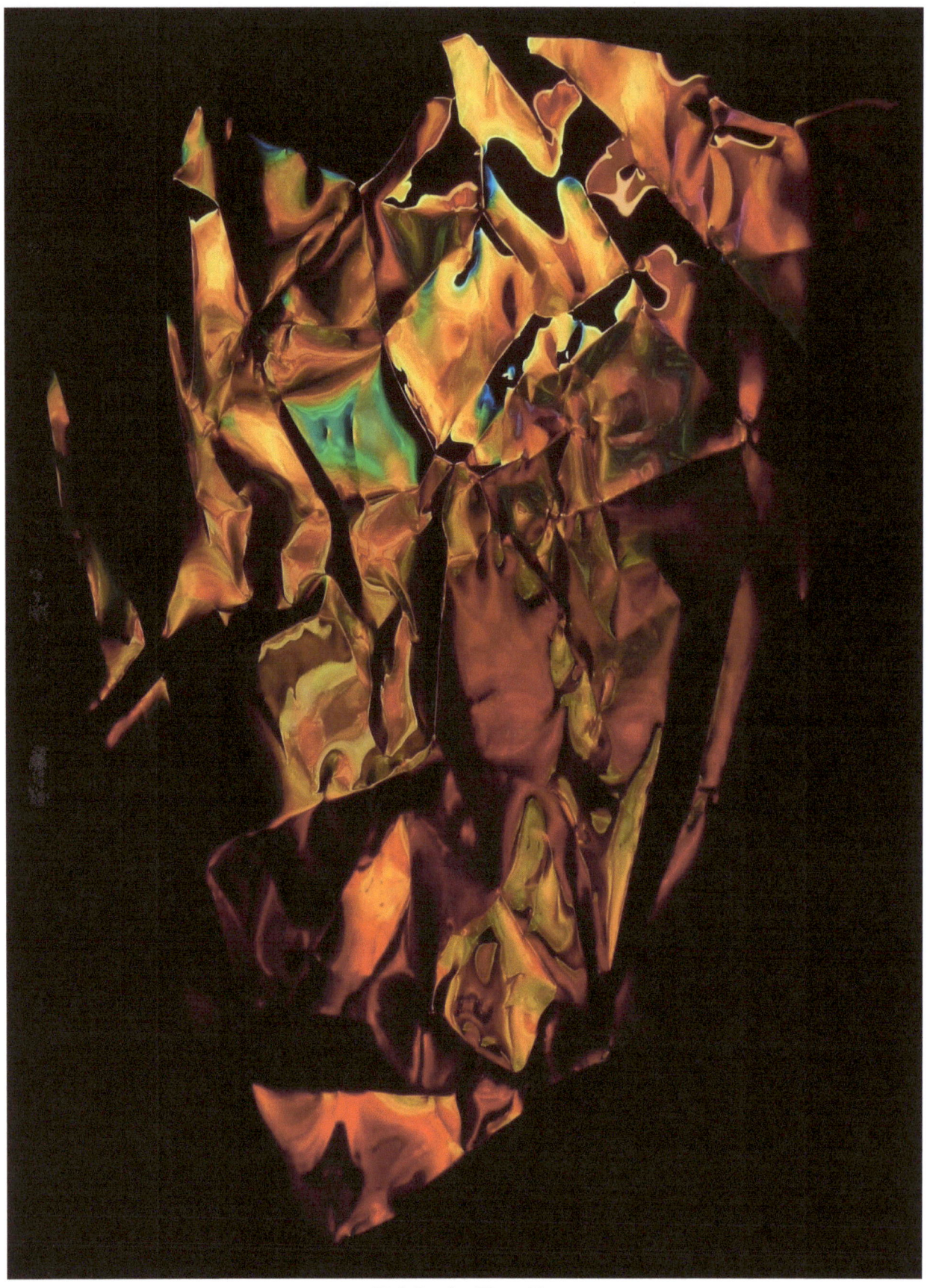

Didn't Do It

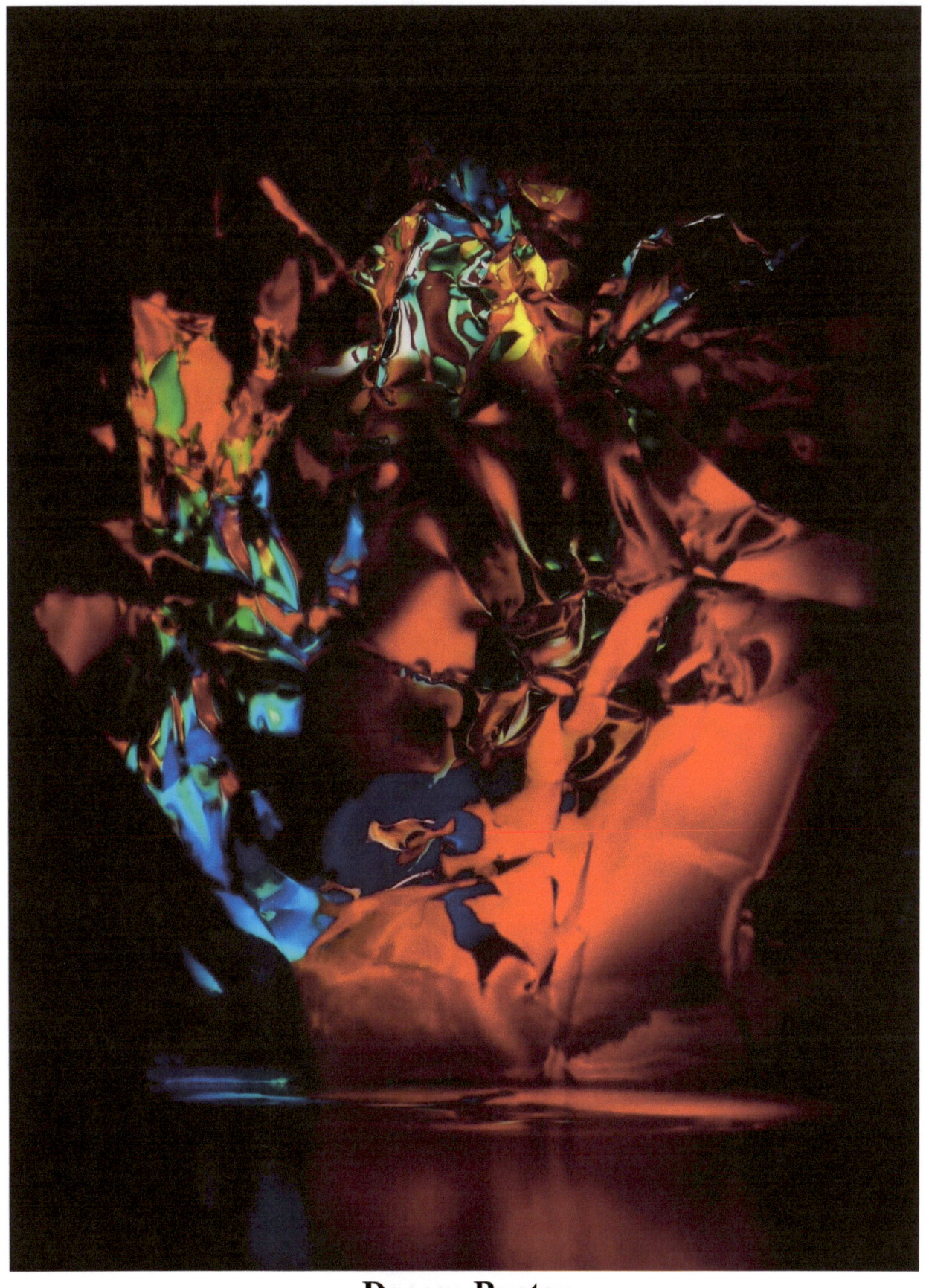

Dream Buster

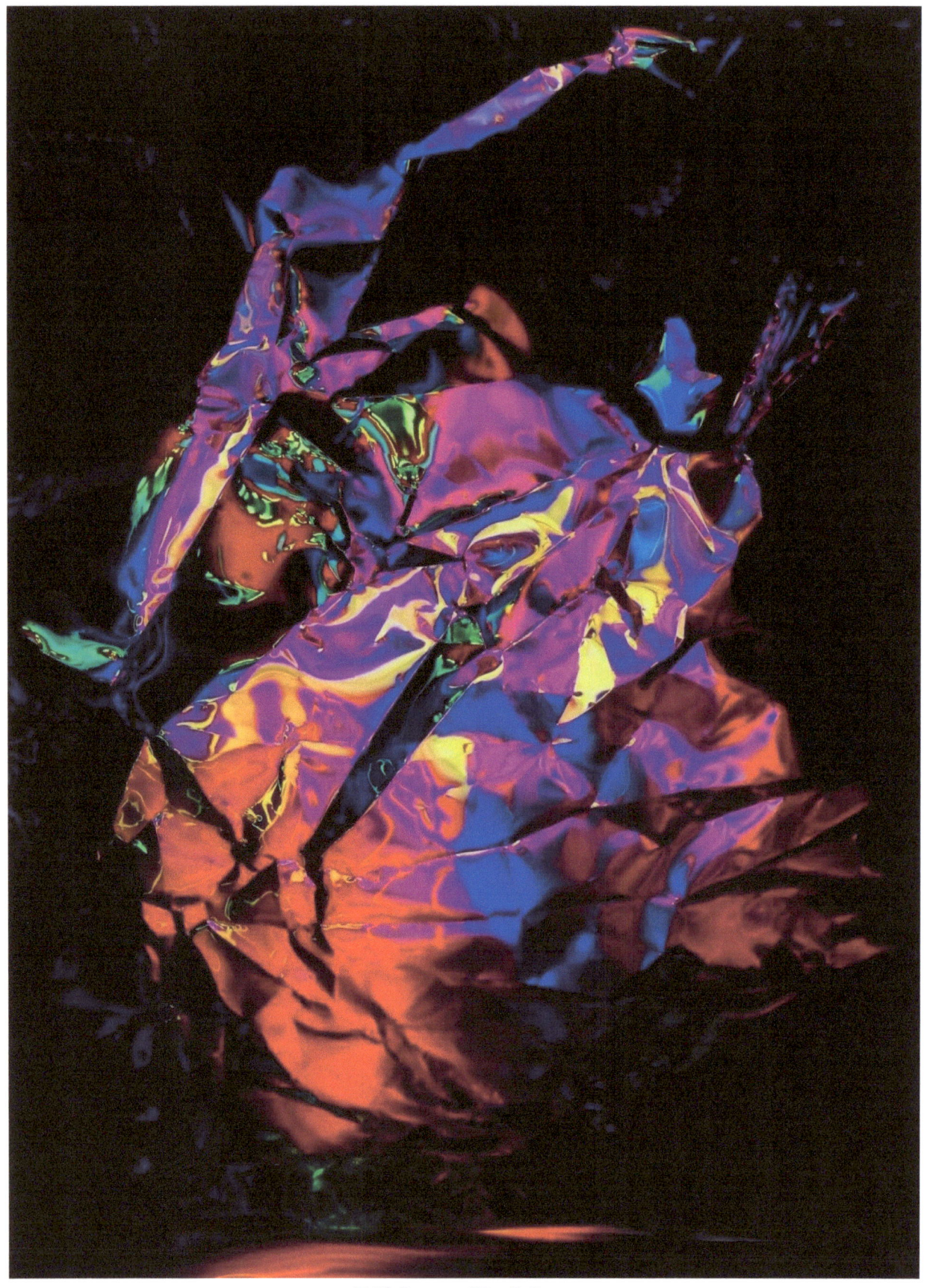

Kidney Bolder

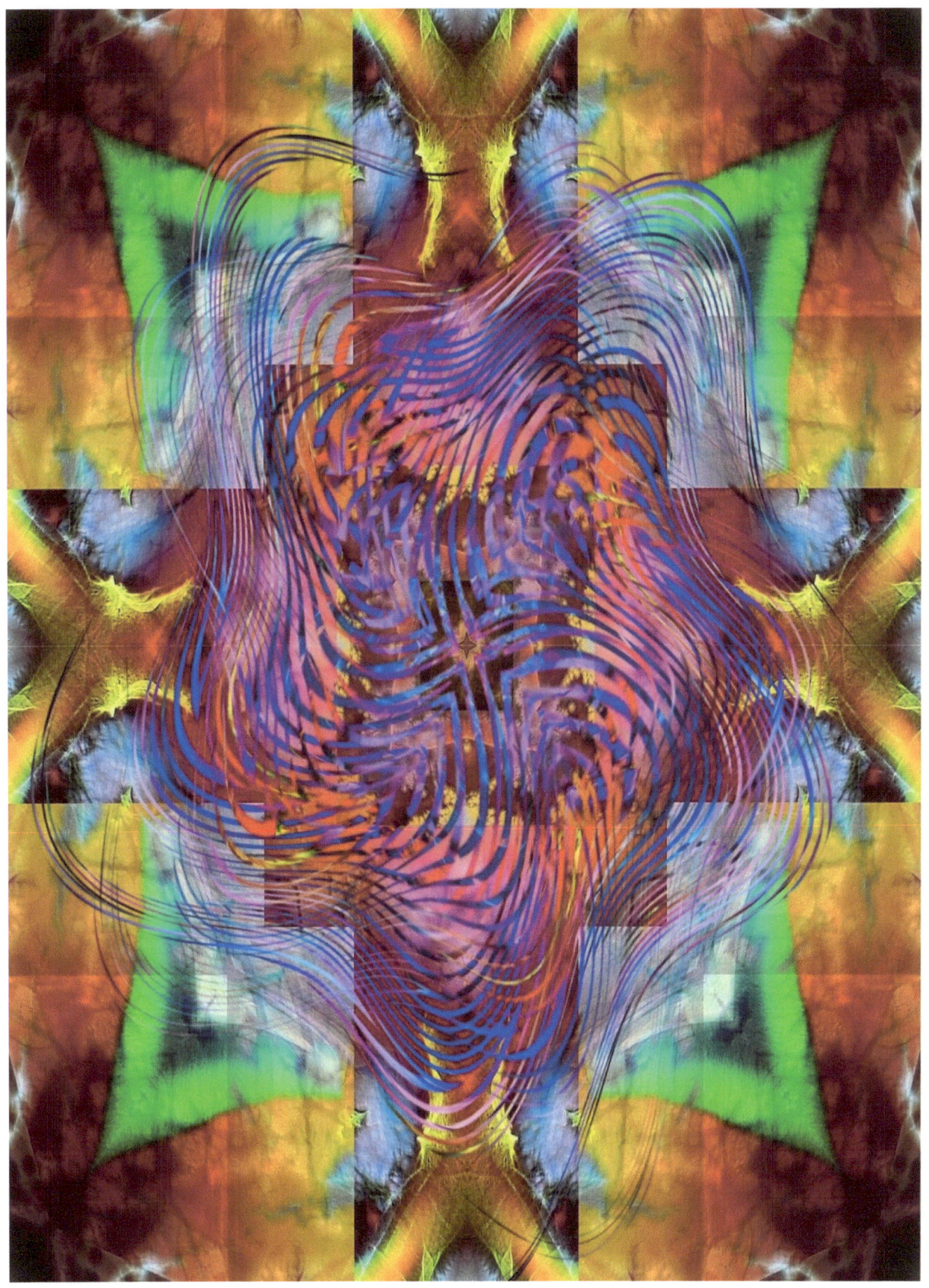

Abrasive Quiet

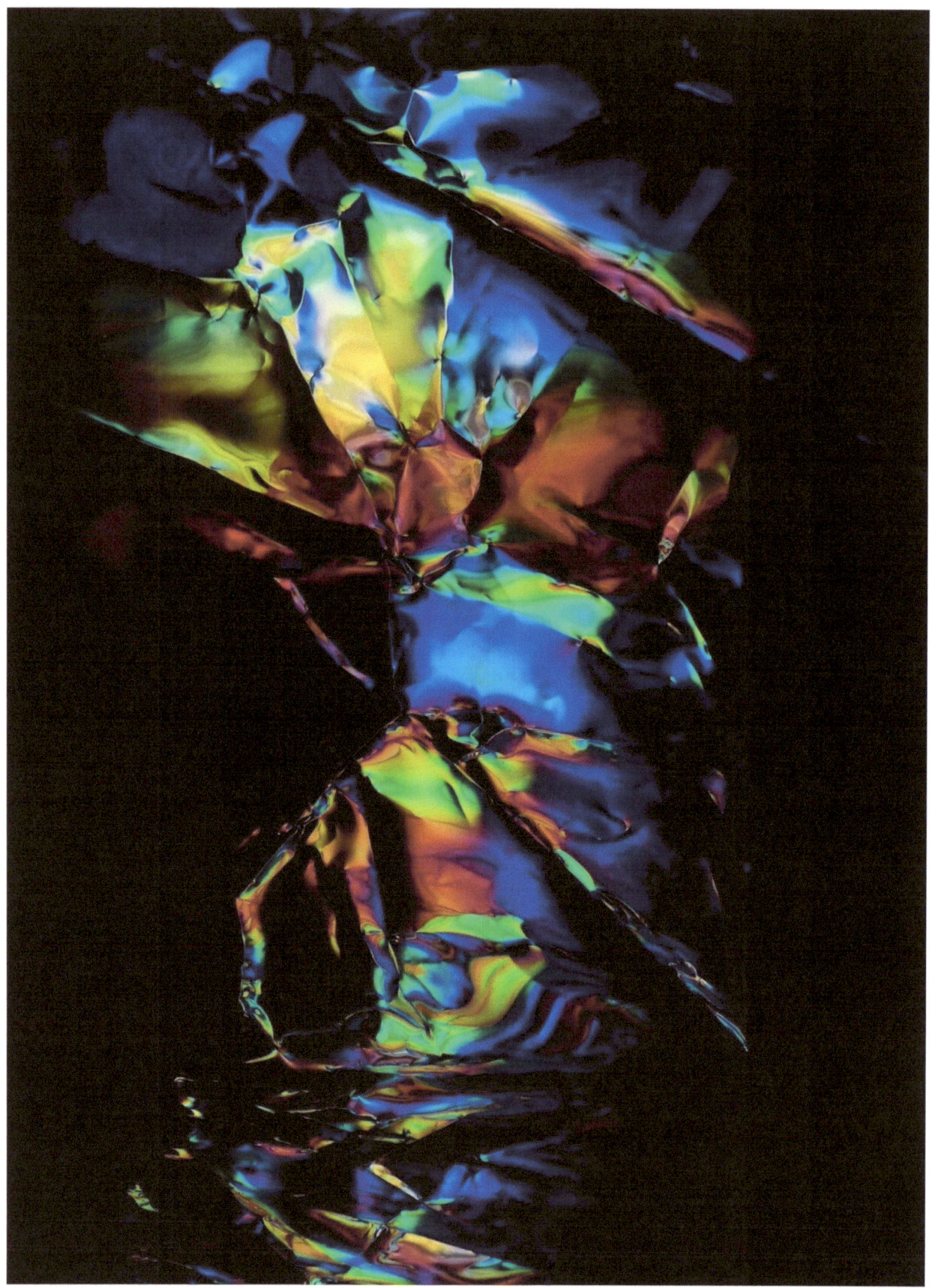

Long Wait

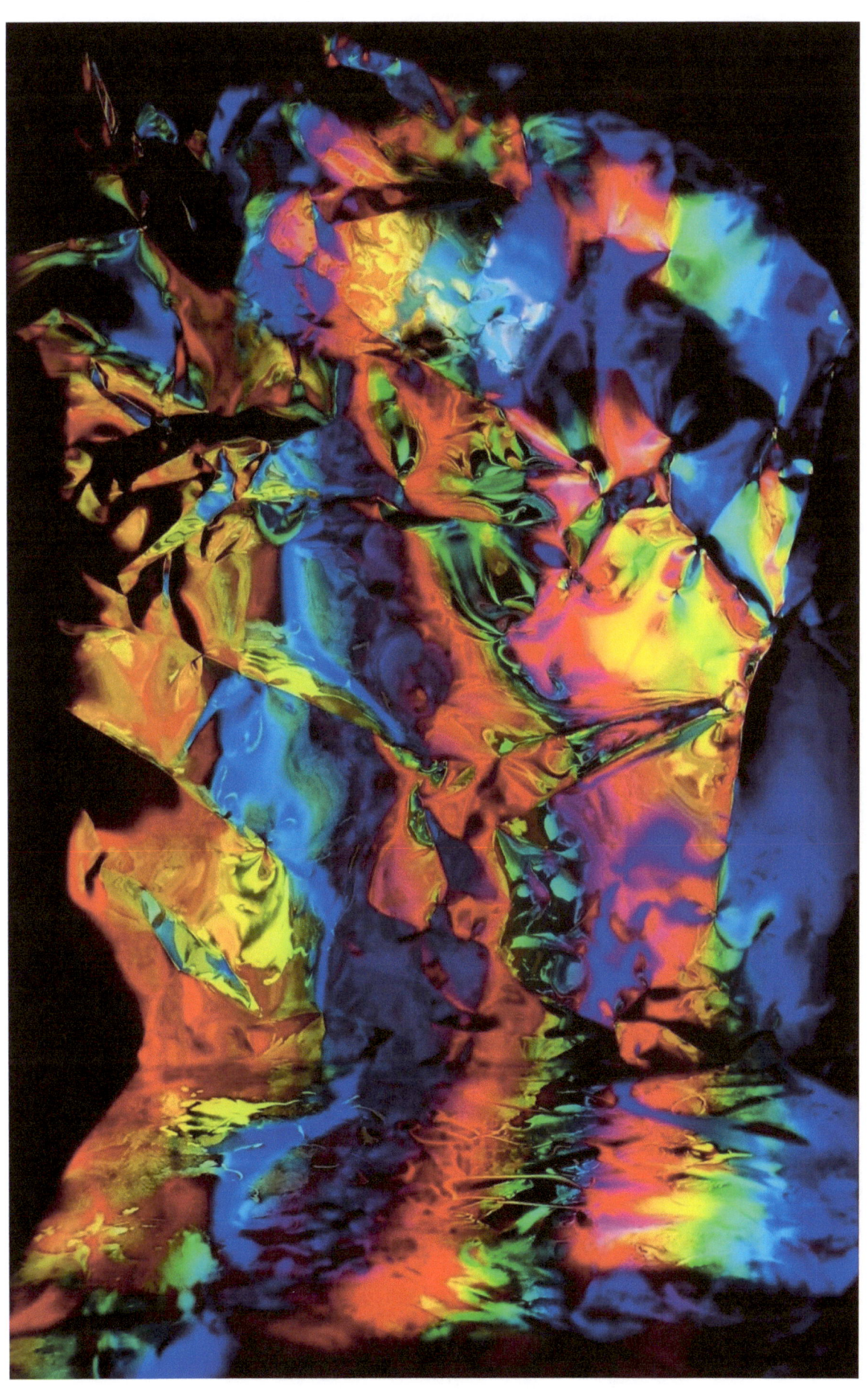

Reality 92

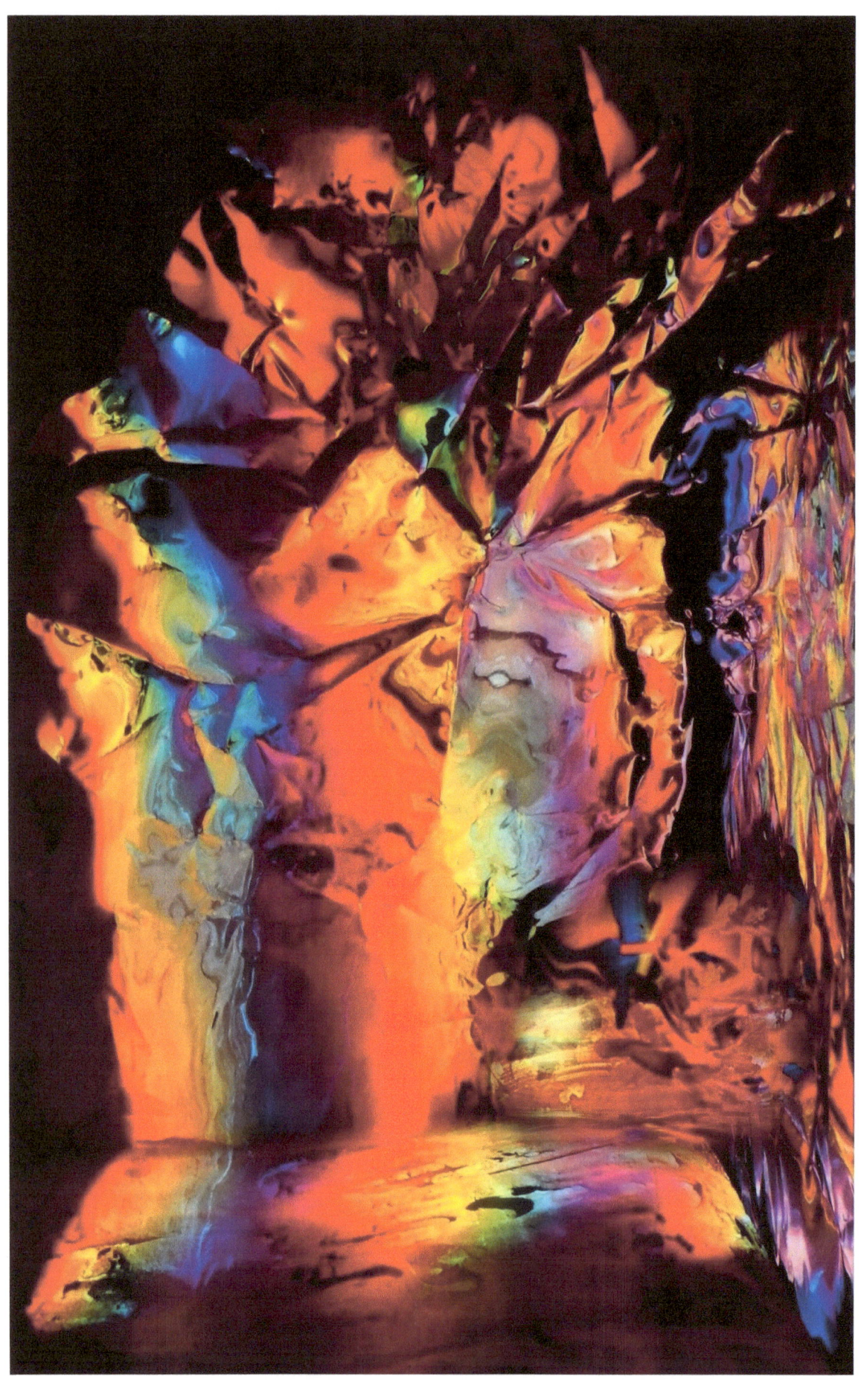

So What?

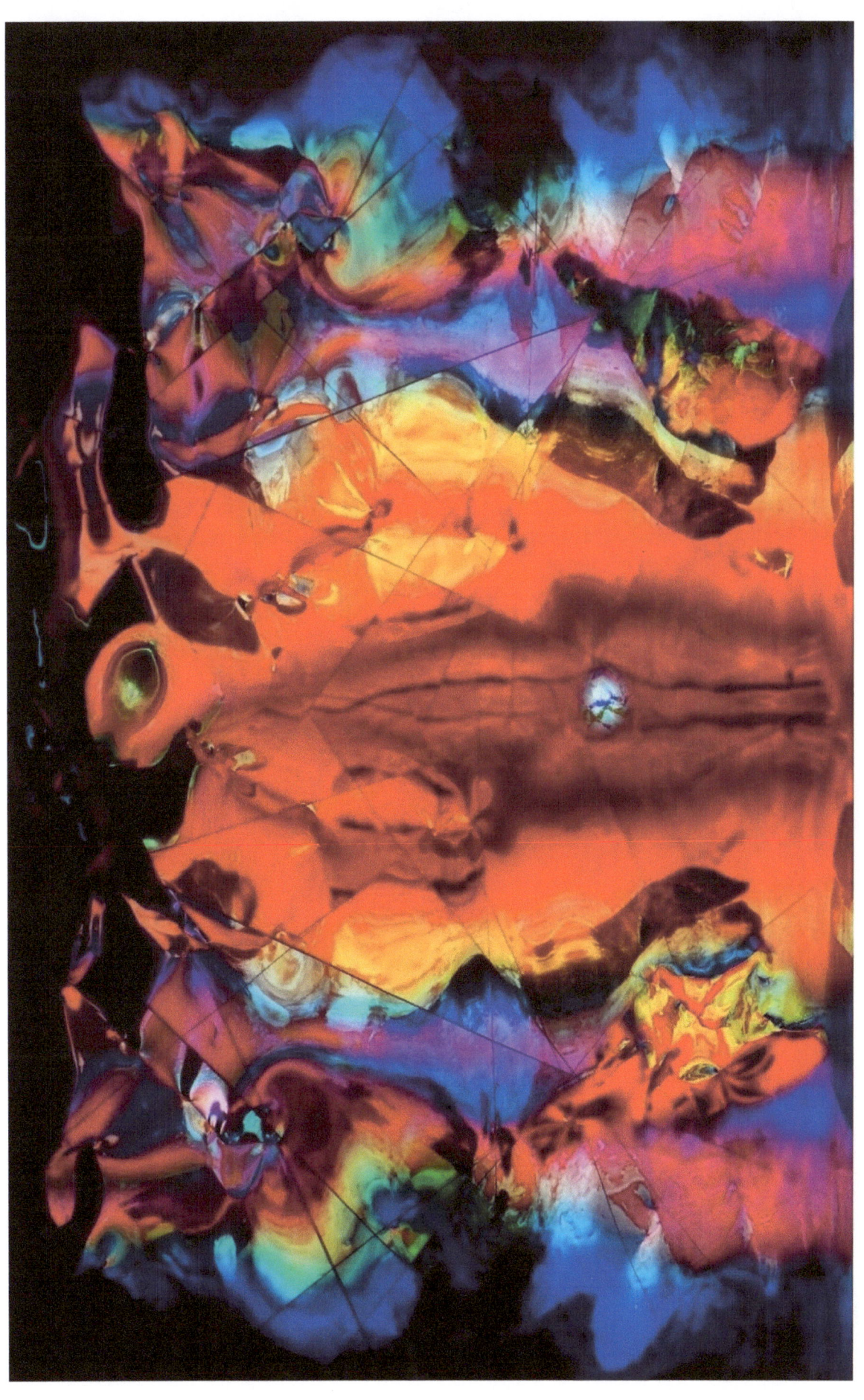

Theme of Sinews

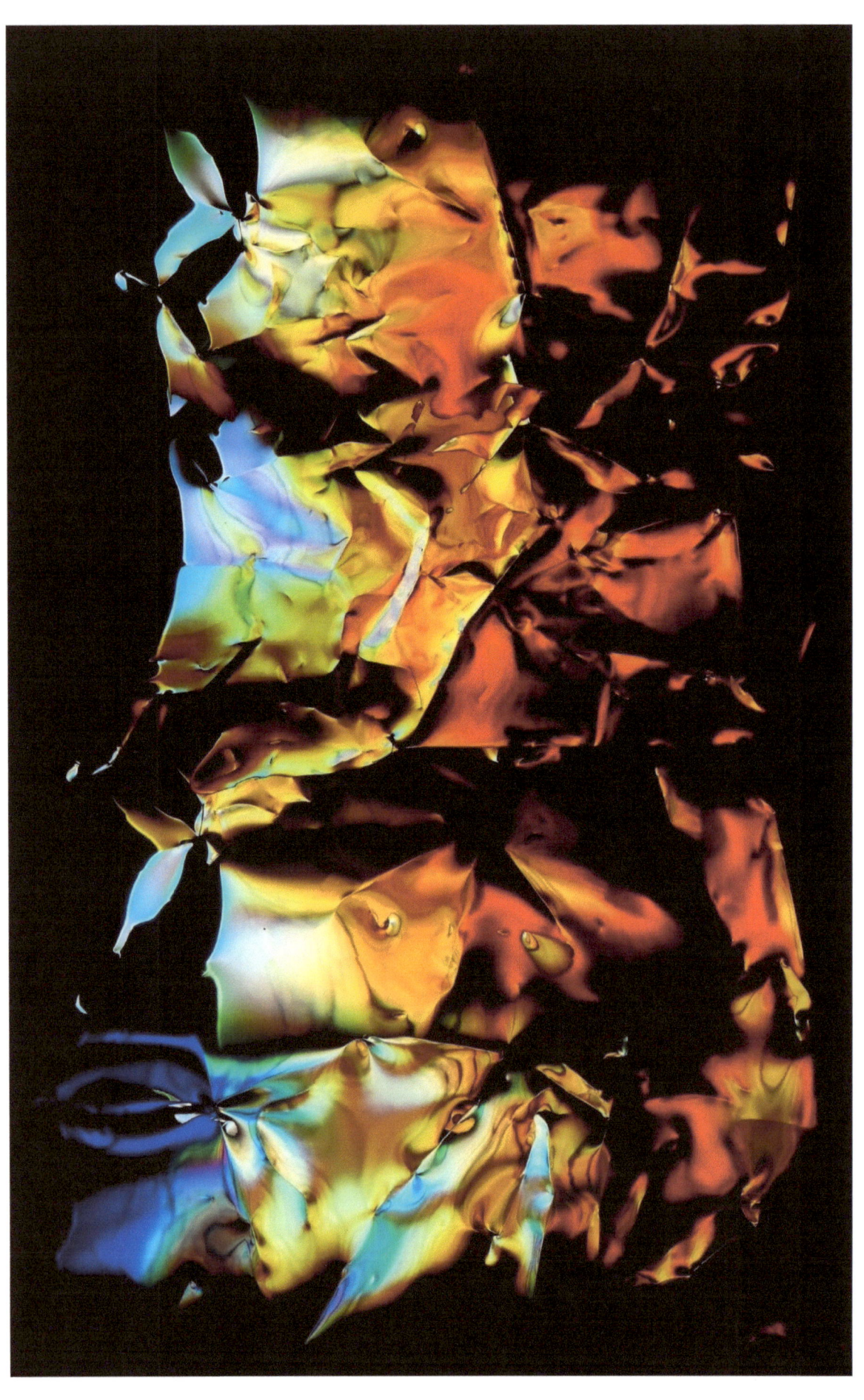

Squares Rounds

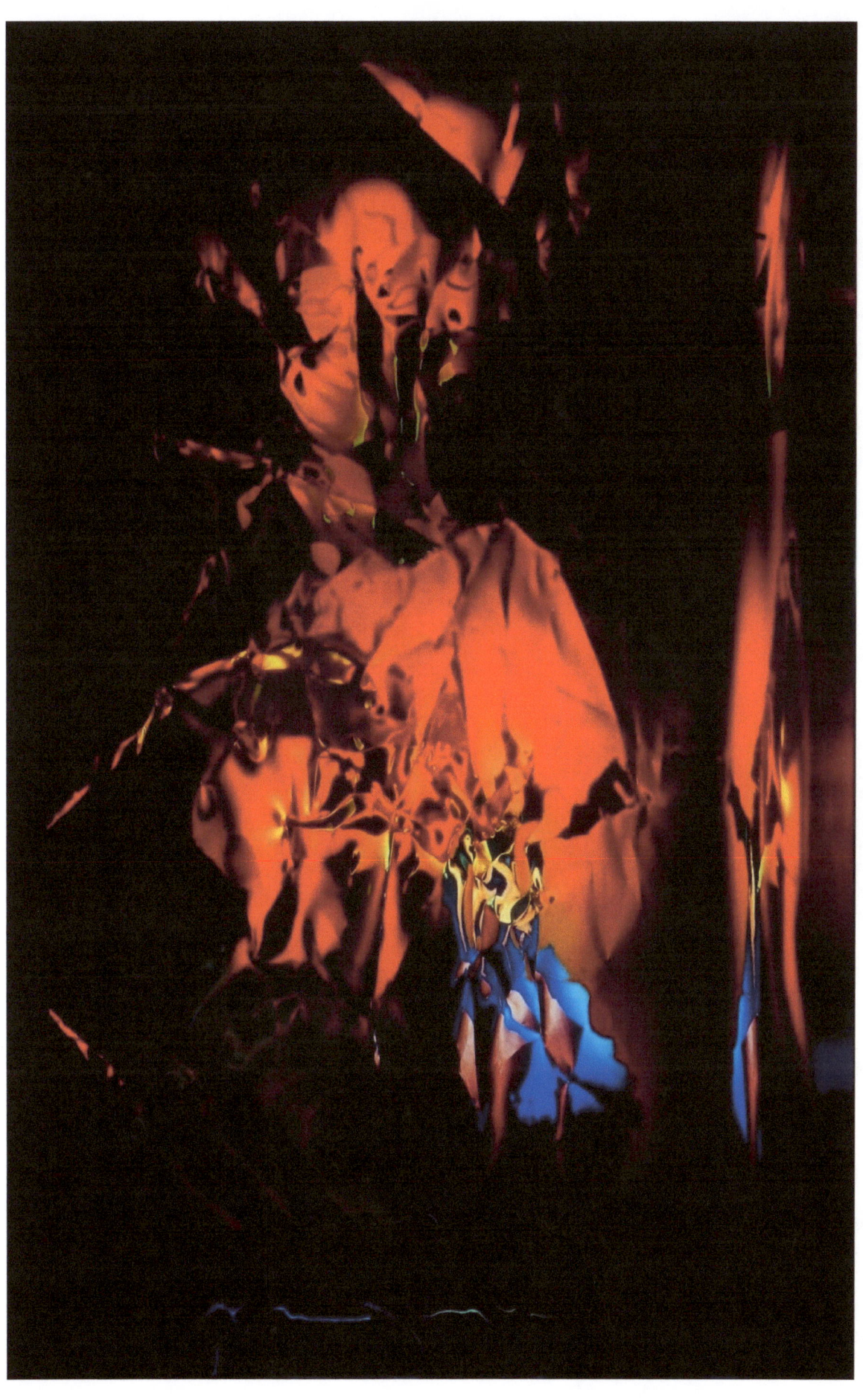

Unexpected

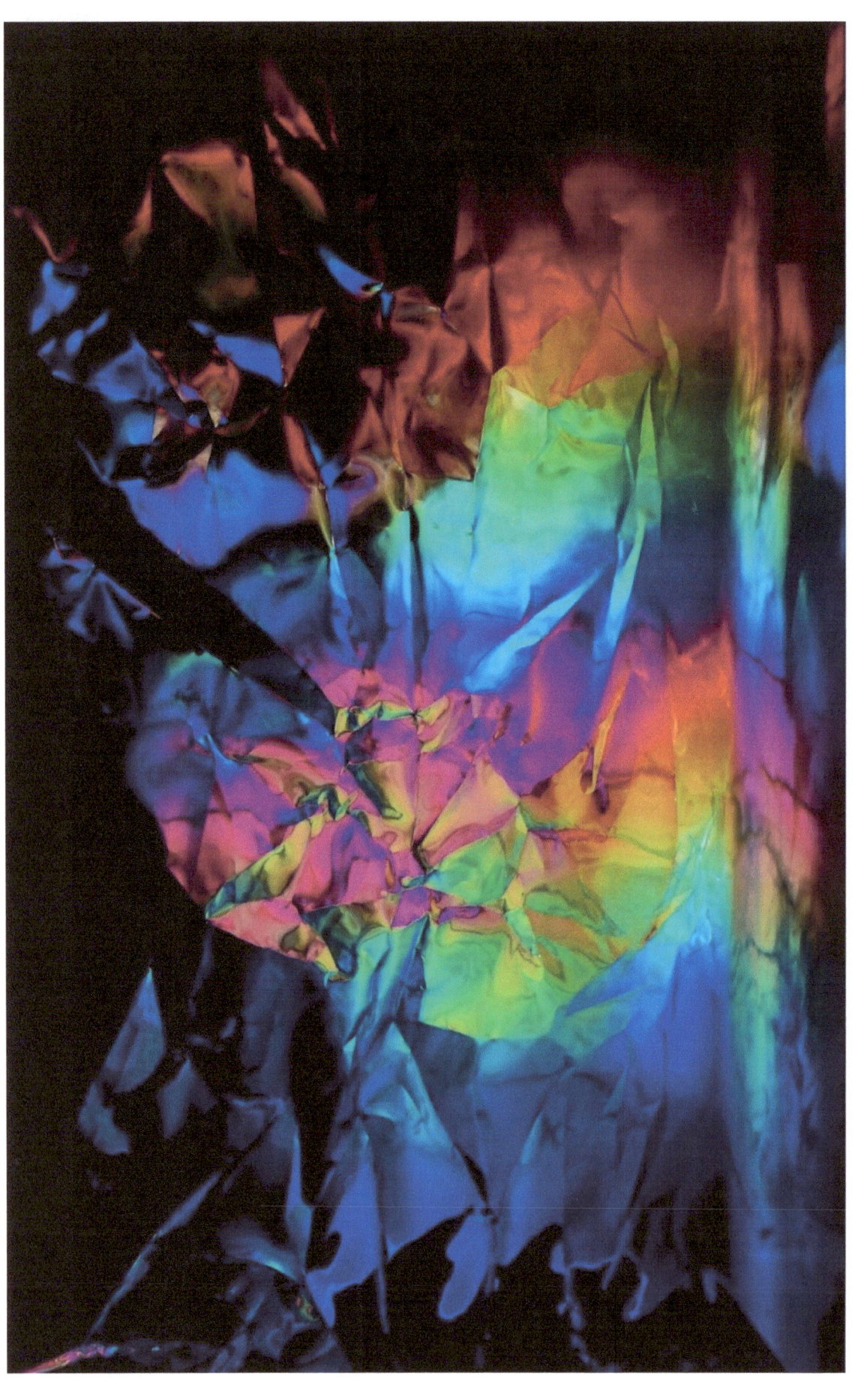

Substantial Ism

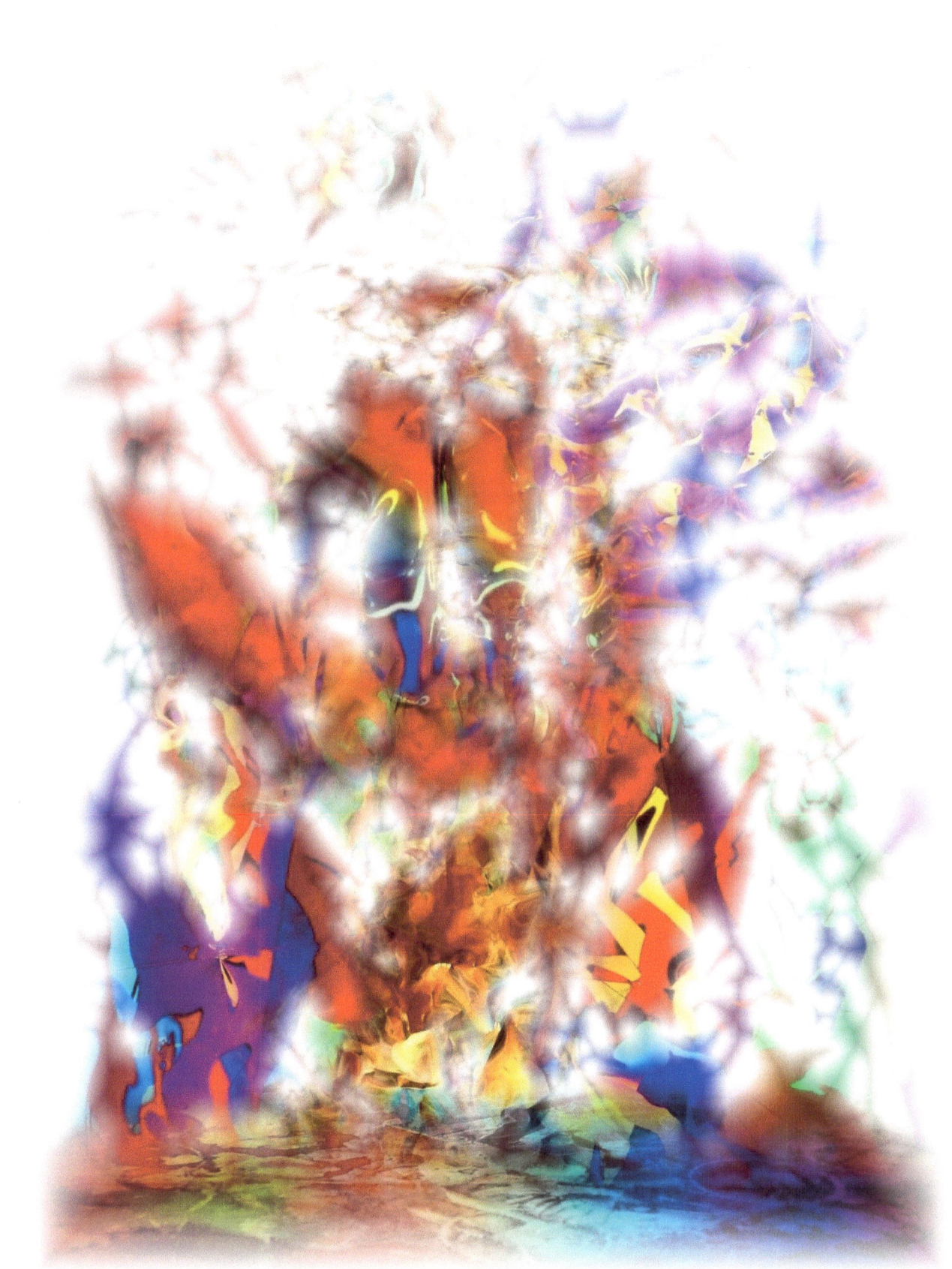

www.ingramcontent.com/pod-product-compliance
Lightning Source LLC
Chambersburg PA
CBHW040754200526
45159CB00025B/2093